T0374361

Modeling and Simulation of Complex Collective Systems

Providing a comprehensive overview of the modeling of complex systems, with particular emphasis on the collective aspects of these systems, this book situates itself at the forefront of available literature. Exemplifying practically Wolfram's theses found in *A New Kind of Science*, discussions center on where it is best to use a cellular automaton, when it is reasonable to use a hybrid approach, and when it is best to use a traditional method such as one based on differential equations.

A range of fascinating examples are discussed, from models of crowd dynamics to car traffic, downhill skiers, and oil spreading across the sea surface. All are discussed and illustrated with comments. These examples explore how simple rules can create incredibly complex patterns and are used to compare cellular automata with more traditional methods.

This book is of critical importance to students and lecturers interested in complex system modeling as well as containing translatable techniques that have applications in a wide range of fields.

Jarosław Wąs' area of research is among complex systems: crowd and vehicle dynamics, making decisions process, artificial life, and data-driven simulations of collective systems. He has authored many publications in the areas of computer science and artificial intelligence. He currently serves as the director of the Applied Computer Science Department at AGH University of Science and Technology in Kraków, Poland.

Modeling and Simulation of Complex Collective Systems

Jarosław Wąs

CRC Press
Taylor & Francis Group
Boca Raton London New York

CRC Press is an imprint of the
Taylor & Francis Group, an **Informa** business

First edition published 2024
by CRC Press
6000 Broken Sound Parkway NW, Suite 300, Boca Raton, FL 33487-2742

and by CRC Press
4 Park Square, Milton Park, Abingdon, Oxon, OX14 4RN

CRC Press is an imprint of Taylor & Francis Group, LLC

© 2024 Jarosław Wąs

Reasonable efforts have been made to publish reliable data and information, but the author and publisher cannot assume responsibility for the validity of all materials or the consequences of their use. The authors and publishers have attempted to trace the copyright holders of all material reproduced in this publication and apologize to copyright holders if permission to publish in this form has not been obtained. If any copyright material has not been acknowledged please write and let us know so we may rectify in any future reprint.

Except as permitted under U.S. Copyright Law, no part of this book may be reprinted, reproduced, transmitted, or utilized in any form by any electronic, mechanical, or other means, now known or hereafter invented, including photocopying, microfilming, and recording, or in any information storage or retrieval system, without written permission from the publishers.

For permission to photocopy or use material electronically from this work, access www.copyright.com or contact the Copyright Clearance Center, Inc. (CCC), 222 Rosewood Drive, Danvers, MA 01923, 978-750-8400. For works that are not available on CCC please contact mpkbookspermissions@tandf.co.uk

Trademark notice: Product or corporate names may be trademarks or registered trademarks and are used only for identification and explanation without intent to infringe.

ISBN: 978-1-032-53900-3 (hbk)
ISBN: 978-1-032-54224-9 (pbk)
ISBN: 978-1-003-41580-0 (ebk)

DOI: 10.1201/b23388

Typeset in CMR10
by KnowledgeWorks Global Ltd.

Publisher's note: This book has been prepared from camera-ready copy provided by the authors.

Contents

List of Figures ix

List of Tables xv

Acronyms xvii

1 Introduction 1
  1.1 Motivation – Collective Aspects of Complex Systems 1
  1.2 Related Previous Research 3
  1.3 Book Content Layout 5
  Bibliography 6

2 Cellular Automata 11
  2.1 Definition of Cellular Automata 11
    2.1.1 Elementary Cellular Automata 12
    2.1.2 Characteristic Examples of Classic Cellular Automata 16
  2.2 Different Types of Cellular Automata 20
  2.3 Lattice Gas Automata 22
  2.4 Extensions of the Concept of Cellular Automata 24
  Bibliography 25

3 Crowd Dynamics and Behavior 27
  3.1 Basics of Modeling of Crowd Dynamics and Behavior 27
    3.1.1 Macroscopic Approach 29
    3.1.2 Microscopic Approach 31
  3.2 Molecular Dynamics-Based Approach 32
  3.3 Cellular Automata-Based Approach 34
  3.4 Discrete Agent-Based Models of Crowd Dynamics 35
    3.4.1 Agent-Based Approach in Crowd Modeling 36
  3.5 Selected Applications of Crowd Dynamics Models 40
    3.5.1 Lecture Rooms – Case Study 40
    3.5.2 The Municipal Stadium in Krakow – Case Study . . . 40
    3.5.3 Allianz Arena Munich – Case Study 42
  3.6 Verification and Validation 47
  3.7 Discussion 47
  Bibliography 48

4 Car Traffic Modeling   **51**
    4.1   Basics of Modeling and Simulation of Car Traffic   51
          4.1.1   Road Traffic Measurements and Basic Concepts   51
          4.1.2   Existing Approaches in Car Traffic Modeling   52
    4.2   Proposed Traffic Model   54
          4.2.1   Basic Assumptions of the Proposed Model   55
          4.2.2   Proposed Modification of the Rules of the Na-Sch Model   57
          4.2.3   Movement Algorithm   58
          4.2.4   Measurement of Traffic Volumes   63
          4.2.5   Calculation Time with Increased Traffic Volume . . .   65
    4.3   Verification and Validation   66
    4.4   Discussion   67
    Bibliography   68

5 Modeling Dynamics of Downhill Skiers   **71**
    5.1   Basics of Modeling and Simulation of Skiing   71
    5.2   How to Model Skiers' Dynamics   73
          5.2.1   Way-Point Forces   74
          5.2.2   Neighbor Repulsion Forces   74
          5.2.3   Obstacle Repulsion Forces   76
          5.2.4   Slope Edge Repulsion Forces   77
          5.2.5   Characteristics of Physical Forces in Skiing   79
    5.3   Sample Simulations of Downhill Skiing   81
          5.3.1   Parameters of Skiers and Physical Constants   81
          5.3.2   Characteristics of Ski Lifts   82
          5.3.3   Sample Results of Simulations   83
    5.4   Verification and Validation   86
    5.5   Discussion   86
    Bibliography   87

6 Oil Spill Modeling   **89**
    6.1   Basics of Modeling and Simulation of Oil Spill   89
          6.1.1   Processes Associated with Oil Spills   90
    6.2   Selected Methods of Oil Spill Modeling   92
    6.3   Hybrid Approach in Oil Spill Modeling   93
          6.3.1   Basic Elements of the Model   94
          6.3.2   Algorithm of the Hybrid Oil Spill Model   94
    6.4   Component Processes in the Spreading of Oil Spills   95
          6.4.1   Advection   97
          6.4.2   Spreading   98
          6.4.3   Evaporation   100
          6.4.4   Emulsification   100
          6.4.5   Changes in the Oil Density – Evaporation and
                  Emulsification   101
          6.4.6   Natural Dispersion   101

6.4.7 Viscosity of Oil as a Dynamic Process 102

6.4.8 Interaction with the Seashore 102

6.5 Simulation of Oil Spills 103

6.5.1 An Example – Deepwater Horizon 2010 104

6.6 Verification and Validation 104

6.7 Discussion 106

Bibliography 107

7 Summary **111**

Index **113**

List of Figures

1.1   The relationship between theory, model, and simulation. . . .   2

1.2   Development and assessment of simulations.   2

1.3   Sample flowchart of model assessment to evaluate production versions of complex system applications.   3

2.1   From a set of rules to Elementary Cellular Automata.   13

2.2   Elementary CA - rule 15   14

2.3   Example of class 1 of cellular automaton – rule 222 of ECA .   14

2.4   Example of class 2 of cellular automaton – rule 190 of ECA .   15

2.5   Example of class 3 of cellular automaton – rule 30 of ECA . .   15

2.6   Example of class 4 of cellular automaton – rule 110 of ECA .   16

2.7   On the left, the initial configuration of a Gosper Glider Gun – a characteristic configuration of Conway's Game of Life. On the right simulation after 27 steps – the first movable structure was formed a glider. (a) Gosper Glider Gun – step 0. (b) Gosper Glider Gun – step 27.   17

2.8   On the left simulation of a Gosper Glider Gun. Two movable structures gliders are visible. On the right, cyclically generated structures, gliders, are visible. (a) Gosper Glider Gun – step 71. (b) Gosper Glider Gun – step 91.   17

2.9   On the left – initial phase of Langton's Ant walking – the initial phase of chaotic wandering. On the right – simulation after 7000 steps – visible characteristic traces in the phase of chaotic wandering. (a) Langton's Ant – step 100. (b) Lanton's Ant – step 7000.   18

2.10 On the left – visible maximum growth of the structure in the phase of chaotic wandering. On the right – a surprising change in the resulting structure created, after about 10000 steps of chaotic wandering, a regular structure called highway begins to be created. (a) Langton's Ant – step 10000. (b) Langton's Ant – step 11000.   19

2.11 Langton's Ant – step 20000 – the constantly expanding highway structure is visible.   19

2.12 Two popular neighborhoods defined for 2D Cellular Automata with a square lattice. (a) von Neumann neighborhood. (b) Moore neighborhood.   20

2.13 Two consecutive phases of Margolus neighborhood defined for
      2D Cellular Automata with a square lattice.   21
2.14 Hexagonal lattice with three characteristic types of neighbor-
      hood. (a) Tripod neighborhood scheme. (b) Honey neighbor-
      hood scheme. (c) Hexagonal star neighborhood scheme. . . .   21
2.15 Characteristics of the HPP and FHP methods. (a) Collision
      scheme for the HPP model. (b) Collision scheme for the FHP
      model.   23

3.1   Types of crowd – according to Forsyth [3].   28
3.2   Decision-making by pedestrians represented by agents.   28
3.3   Scales in pedestrians modeling including micro-scale – particu-
      lar pedestrians/agents, meso-scale – groups of pedestrians, and
      macro-scale – the whole crowd.   29
3.4   Six basic levels of services taking into account available space
      for a single pedestrian in a considered scenario according to
      John J. Fruin [9].   30
3.5   Mechanism of superposition of forces in the Social Force Model.
      Group of pedestrians head toward POI A (Point of Interest A),
      while a pedestrian heads toward POI B (Point of Interest B).
      The figure shows the main types of forces acting in the system
      for a normal situation.   32
3.6   Transition matrix for Cellular Automata-based models of
      crowds for a neighborhood with the radius $R = 1$. On the left,
      the von Neumann neighborhood, on the right, the Moore neigh-
      borhood.   35
3.7   Examples of basic grids and floor fields: Lattice with moving
      pedestrians, static floor fields with POIs, obstacle floor field,
      dynamic floor field (using an analogy to the chemotaxis pro-
      cess), and proxemic floor field.   36
3.8   Popular 2D representations of pedestrians. On the left, two
      square representations and a hexagonal representation. On the
      right, elliptical representations of Social Distances Model pro-
      posed in [18] and a general case with an adaptive size.   37
3.9   General view on tactical and operational phase in the movement
      algorithm using static and dynamic floor fields (dynamic floor
      field is denoted as dyn FF).   39
3.10 Evacuation scenario from the U2 learning center of AGH Uni-
      versity of Science and Technology. On the left, experiments with
      students; on the right, view of agent-based simulation. (a) Evac-
      uated agents are allocated in the simulation environment. (b)
      Trajectories of evacuated agents.   41
3.11 Statistics of frequency in particular cells during evacuation are
      visualized.   42

3.12 Non-competitive evacuation scenario of leaving the stands of the Municipal Stadium in Krakow. (a) Collecting empirical data – two neighboring sectors in the stadium with evacuated fans are visible. Competitive behaviors are not observed. (b) Simulation applied for sectors – the warmer the color, the longer evacuation time from a particular seat 43

3.13 Distribution of average speed and evacuated persons in time. Statistics for a non-competitive evacuation scenario of leaving the east stands of the Municipal Stadium Krakow. 43

3.14 Simulation server – scheme for modeling of the Allianz Arena Munich stadium. 44

3.15 Simulation of pedestrian flow in the Allianz Arena Munich stadium, using a modified Social Distances Model. 44

3.16 Sample statistics for flow in the stands of Allianz Arena Munich are presented: frequency matrix of flowing agents for the three following scenarios: (a) normal situation – low fluctuations, (b) non-competitive evacuation – moderate fluctuations, and (c) competitive evacuation – high fluctuations. 45

3.17 Simulation of pedestrian flow in Allianz Arena Munich stadium, using modified Social Distances Model – normal situation. . . 45

3.18 Simulation of pedestrian flow in Allianz Arena Munich stadium, using modified Social Distances Model – non-competive situation. 46

3.19 Simulation of pedestrian flow in Allianz Arena Munich stadium, using modified Social Distances Model – competitive situation. 46

3.20 Fundamental diagram of pedestrian flow in a modified Social Distances Model used for the simulation of crowds for stadium scenarios. Compressibility factor Eps = 0.0. Reference diagrams: SFPE – Society of Fire Protection Engineers, PM – Predtetschenski and Milinski, WM – Weidemann. 48

4.1 Sample configuration of cars in consecutive time steps in the Nagel-Schreckenberg model. 53

4.2 Representation of space and vehicles in the proposed model. . 55

4.3 Distance d as the distance between two driving vehicles c_1 and c_2 and distance d_{real} as the sum of d and the sudden braking distance of the vehicle c_2. 57

4.4 Graphical representation of the obstacle search by the vehicle c_1 – two obstacles were found: the vehicle driving in front p_1 and the blocked cell of a special type (p_2). 58

4.5 View on intersection representation using traffic lights, including a conditional green arrow, check point, and priority point. 59

4.6 A complex intersection including a sample cycle of traffic lights. 60

4.7 An entering mechanism for road connections. 60

4.8 A crossing point mechanism for road connections.   61
4.9 Change line mechanism.   61
4.10 Simulation setup – road. An example of Opolska Street in
     Krakow.   62
4.11 Simulation setup – road configurations with allocated car gener-
     ators. An example of the city of Kraków (Azory/Prądnik Biały
     Districts).   62
4.12 Sample simulation screen for Opolska Street (intersection with
     Wyki Street). The current status of lights with passing vehicles
     is displayed.   63
4.13 Location of measuring points where the vehicle flow was mea-
     sured – city of Kraków (Azory/Prądnik Biały Districts). . . .   63
4.14 Traffic volume measurement for Conrada street at checkpoint
     a. (a) $J(\rho)$ for $p_{break} = 0.15$. (b) $v(\rho)$ for $p_{break} = 0.15$. (c) $v(J)$
     for $p_{break} = 0.15$.   64
4.15 Traffic volume measurement for Opolska street at checkpoint b.
     (a) $J(\rho)$ for $p_{break} = 0.15$. (b) $v(\rho)$ for $p_{break} = 0.15$. (c) $v(J)$
     for $p_{break} = 0.15$.   64
4.16 Traffic volume measurement for Krowoderskich Zuchów Street
     at checkpoint c. (a) $J(\rho)$ for $p_{break} = 0.15$. (b) $v(\rho)$ for $p_{break} =$
     0.15. (c) $v(J)$ for $p_{break} = 0.15$.   65
4.17 Graph showing the dependence of the calculation time on the
     number of vehicles   66
4.18 Fundamental diagrams from experiments. $J(\rho)$, $V(\rho)$, and $v(J)$,
     where $J_{max} \approx 1800 \frac{vehicles}{hour} \rho_{max} \approx 170 \frac{vehicles}{hour}$. (a) Relationship
     speed vs. density. (b) Relationship speed vs. specific flow. (c)
     Relationship between specific flow and density.   67

5.1 The sense and direction of the centripetal force depending on
     the turn stage.   72
5.2 Two main types of turns in skiing: skidded and curved. (a)
     Mechanism of skidded turns. (b) Mechanism of curved turns.   72
5.3 The current direction of movement e and desired direction
     e_{social} is greater than δ; thus, the skier will perform a right
     turn.   73
5.4 Social Forces of particular skiers.   74
5.5 Social ellipse of skier α.   75
5.6 Social ellipse of skier α for different values of current speed. .   76
5.7 Repulsion forces between skiers according to [5].   77
5.8 Forces acting on a skier.   79
5.9 Characteristic of centrifugal and lateral forces depending on the
     turning phase.   81
5.10 The main parameters applied during simulation.   82

5.11 The first run of simulation. The following parameters are applied: total number of skiers: 100, $f_c = 0.05$, and $f_{c-turning} = 0.06$. (a) Statistics of medium speeds. (b) Statistics of most visited places. (c) Statistics of mean distances between skiers.   83

5.12 Second simulation run. Number of skiers: 100, $f_c = 0.03$, and $f_{c-turning} = 0.04$. (a) Chart of medium speeds. (b) Chart of most visited points. (c) Chart of mean distances between skiers.   84

5.13 Relationship between the number of skiers and lift capacity. .   85

5.14 Relationship between the number of skiers and average speed.   85

5.15 Comparison of simulated trajectory in the last part of the slope with a length of about 270 m. (a) The line indicates the trajectory of a randomly selected skier. Points map the positions of obstacles. (b) The visible lines indicate the most common trajectory of movement.   86

6.1 Oil spill processes.   91

6.2 Hybrid approach in oil spill modeling: Cells of Cellular Automata with Oil Point States (OPS) including Oil Particles. .   95

6.3 Algorithm of the hybrid model.   96

6.4 Algorithm of spreading process.   99

6.5 The Deepwater Horizon oil spill: the oil imprint on the water surface – (left) real data from the DWH oil spill [41–43] – 25 April 2010 versus the presented model (right) – a sketch with visible impact on the waterfront area.   104

6.6 Comparison of different characteristics for: ADIOS2, experimental data, Sebastiao & Soares model, and proposed hybrid model.   105

List of Tables

2.1 Definition of Cellular Automata According to J. R. Weimar . 12

4.1 Velocity Values for the Interval Equal to 500 ms in the Adopted Model. 56

5.1 The Set of Forces Acting on Skiers in a Modified Social Forces Approach. 80

6.1 Scheme of Data Flow in the Simulation. 97

Acronyms

ABM	Agent-Based Modeling
ADAS	Advanced Driver Assistance Systems
BDI	Belief-Desire-Intention
CA	Cellular Automata
CEV	Cell External Variables
CIV	Cell Internal Variables
DFF	Dynamic Floor Field
DWH	Deepwater Horizon
ECA	Elementary Cellular Automata
FHP	Frisch-Hasslacher-Pomeau model
GIS	Geographic Information System
HPP	Hardy-Pomeau-Pazzis model
Na-Sch	Nagel-Schreckenberg Model
FF	Floor Field
ODE	Ordinary Differential Equations
OPs	Oil Particles
OPS	Oil Point State
PDE	Partial Differential Equations
POI	Point of Interest
SFF	Static Floor Field
SFM	Social Force Model

1

Introduction

1.1 Motivation – Collective Aspects of Complex Systems

What is a complex system? According to Hiroki Sayama's definition, *Complex systems are networks made of a number of components that interact with each other, typically in a nonlinear fashion. Complex systems may arise and evolve through self-organization, such that they are neither completely regular nor completely random, permitting the development of emergent behavior at macroscopic scales* [1]. The term complex collective systems (CCS) means complex systems in which the interaction between individual elements is of particular importance [2]. Cellular Automata and agent paradigm are often convenient tools for describing such systems; however, more traditional methods such as Ordinary Differential Equations (ODE) or Partial Differential Equations (PDE) are sometimes used. The cyclical International Workshop on Complex Collective Systems (CCS) as a part of the International Parallel Processing and Applied Mathematics Conference have been organized since 2009 [3] including the following editions: CCS 2009, CCS 2011, CCS 2013, CCS 2015, CCS 2017, CCS 2019, and CCS 2022 [4]. It is an international forum to exchange ideas and present achievements in the field of collective aspects of complex systems [5–7].

To understand the essence of complex systems, two concepts concerning space and time, respectively, are crucial: emergence over scale and self-organization over time. *Emergence* is a word derived from the Greek language, meaning an ascent or emergence concerning a situation where, on the basis of the microscopic properties of a system, we obtain non-trivial macroscopic properties. The term *emergence* therefore denotes a complex and non-trivial relationship between the properties of a system at the microscopic and macroscopic levels. *Self-organization* means a dynamic process, thanks to which the system in question creates non-trivial macroscopic structures or behaviors that evolve over time.

In practice, many tools are used to describe complex systems, including their collective aspects: Ordinary Differential Equations, Partial Differential Equations, queue networks, and, finally, Cellular Automata (CA) and agent systems. Cellular Automata have become very popular in recent years. One of the turning points in the promotion of Cellular Automata was the publication of the book *A New Kind of Science* by Stephan Wolfram. One of Wolfram's

DOI: 10.1201/b23388-1

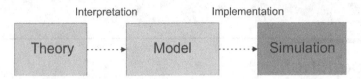

FIGURE 1.1
The relationship between theory, model, and simulation.

main conclusions in this book is that "the universe is discrete in its nature, and runs on fundamental laws which can be described as simple programs" [8]. Wolfram also concluded that the possibilities of describing the world using traditional methods, such as differential equations, are exhausted and the future of modeling belongs to discrete methods such as Cellular Automata. One of the purposes of this book is to address Wolfram's thesis from the perspective of more than 20 years of work in complex system projects and participation in many scientific forums where such work results are presented.

Let us first look at the methodology of modeling and simulation of complex systems. From the point of view of research methodology: models are obtained on the basis of theory interpretation, while the next step is to create computer simulations by means of implementation.

The interpretation should be subject to validation Figure 1.1, i.e., checking whether we have interpreted the theory correctly, while the implementation should be subject to verification (Figure 1.2), i.e. checking whether we have implemented the model correctly [9].

Regarding model assessment, we can use additional mathematical formulas to assess results, i.e., target versions of simulation applications that are to be used in professional applications (e.g., in fire engineering). In this case, the extended version of Figures 1.1. and 1.2. might look like Figure 1.3. The flowchart is inspired by the ISO 16730:2008 standard.

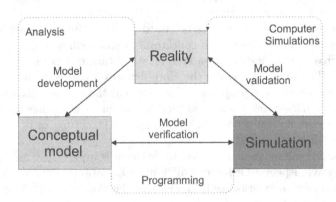

FIGURE 1.2
Development and assessment of simulations.

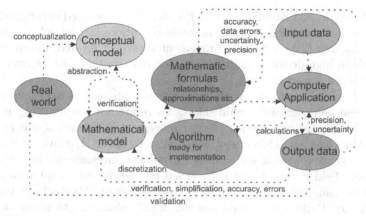

FIGURE 1.3
Sample flowchart of model assessment to evaluate production versions of complex system applications.

1.2 Related Previous Research

Thanks to our Complex Systems Research Group, the Glider Research Group in which I served as a founder and leader, as well as international projects, we have been able to carry out a number of research works related to the modeling of CCS for the last 20-odd years.

Chronologically, the first challenge for me in the modeling of CCS and their collective aspects concerned (and still does) models of crowd dynamics and behavior. We have carried out numerous research studies and developed many models and simulations over the past years. I started from Cellular Automata models of crowds [10, 11] in different conditions together with Bartłomiej Gudowski [12]. Next, we developed a non-homogeneous representation of pedestrians and together with Paweł J. Matuszyk, a hybrid Social Distance Model of pedestrian dynamics [13], as well as a new representation of pedestrians [14]. Another issue considered in the work covered the formal aspects of crowd dynamics described together with Ewa Dudek-Dyduch in [15]. Next, a simulation environment created in Java with Konrad Kułakowski and Paweł Topa [16] was proposed. The application of pedestrian ABMs (agent-based models) for large environments was described together with Robert Lubaś in [17] and [18], as well as issued of proxemics together with Wojciech Myśliwiec [19]. Another issue was the calibration, verification, and validation of crowd models with special focus to procedures dedicated to discrete models, described in cooperation with my former PhD students Jakub Porzycki, Robert Lubaś, and Marcin Mycek [20, 21]. In a publication created with Jakub Porzycki, Leila Hedayatifar, Forough Hassanibesheli, and Krzysztof Kułakowski [22], velocity correlations in unidirectional flow of crowd were analyzed. Together with

Jakub Porzycki and Natalia Schmidt Polończyk, I conducted experimental research on the evacuation of people in smoke conditions [23], as well as extensive survey research [24]. A recently implemented project involves the simulation of people in high-density conditions, carried out together with Dariusz Pałka and Grzegorz Bazior [25, 26].

Another challenge with modeling complex systems was modeling the dynamics and behavior of downhill skiers. There are not many articles relating to complex agent-based models of skier movement [27], hence it was not easy to construct models. This was a task similar to crowd dynamics in terms of people's decision-making and collision avoidance mechanisms. However, the dynamics of skiers' movement is governed by specific rules related to sliding movement using the phenomenon of gravity. I took up this challenge together with Dariusz Pałka and Tomasz Korecki, finally managing to create an effective model of skiers' movement [28].

Another interesting research issue concerning CCS is car traffic, Advanced Driver Assistance Systems (ADAS), or driving autonomous vehicles. In this regard, I also undertook a series of research works. Among the works, one should mention the adaptation of the Nagel-Schreckenberg model to urban conditions. The first series of works was carried out over a dozen years ago and then I created a road traffic simulator based on Cellular Automata together with Rafał Bielinski, Bartłomiej Gajewski, and Patryk Orzechowski [29]. Subsequent works resulted in the expansion of the model using ABM, namely Agent-Based Modeling techniques, and more complex rules of operation – the final model was definitely more realistic and precise [30, 31] – the whole project was carried out together with Magda Chmielewska and Mateusz Kotlarz. Next, together with Krzysztof Małecki and Marek Kamiński, I proposed a model and simulation of traffic including emergency vehicles [32]. Determining the free space boundary in automotive perception systems is an important task from the safety point of view. Together with Marek Szlachetka and Dariusz Borkowski, we proposed a selection methods of parametric curves [33], while the basic environment was described in [34]. The issue of virtual physical models in ADAS was described together with Michał Pikus in [35].

An interesting research issue, which belongs to the phenomena occurring in the world, most often as a result of human activity, is oil spill modeling. In nature, there are phenomena of spontaneous releases of crude oil and gas called oil seep [36]. Experts point out that in the case of natural phenomena, half of the volume of oil gets into the oceans, while the remaining half gets into oil spills as a result of human activity. I carried out a project with Maciej Gług, where we analyzed oil spill mechanisms, and finally, we proposed a model of oil spill release using a combination of the Lagrangian discrete particle algorithm with Cellular Automata [37]. The phenomenon of oil spreading in the marine environment includes a number of component mechanisms such as sea currents, winds, evaporation, natural dispersion, emulsification, and seashore interaction. A very interesting issue was to include all these mechanisms in one framework, taking into account their degree of importance.

Each of the problems presented in this chapter relates to the collective aspects of complex systems. Various practical scientific problems and examples of solutions are presented in this book. I am very grateful to all my collaborators, not only those mentioned in this Introduction but also those I have not mentioned, for the years of cooperation and co-creation of an inspiring scientific environment.

This book is a synthesis of work and achievements in the field of modeling complex systems, which I have proposed and conducted both individually and in teams. In most topics, I was the originator of the research and the framework of algorithms, while individual topics were refined and conducted together with the above-mentioned colleagues, for which I am grateful! This synthesis includes a discussion of the Cellular Automata paradigm, my view on the subject, and finally the presentation of a number of inspiring examples regarding the collective aspects of complex systems.

1.3   Book Content Layout

The structure of this book is as follows:

Chapter 2 discusses the Cellular Automata paradigm as an effective tool for simulating complex systems. First, the definitions and classification of Cellular Automata are presented. Next, Elementary Cellular Automata and various examples of classic two-dimensional Cellular Automata are discussed. Next, attention is paid to Non-homogeneous and Asynchronous Cellular Automata and the concept of hybridization of Cellular Automata is discussed in the sense of their connection with Agent-Based Modeling.

Chapter 3 is a short synthesis of my activities in the field of modeling crowd dynamics. In individual projects, I used and studied various paradigms in the field of crowd dynamics modeling: from differential equations and the application of the principle of superposition of forces, through queuing systems, a cellular automaton using the floor fields scheme, to an agent system based on the extended cellular automaton paradigm. In this chapter, I focus primarily on the latter solution, which has found a number of practical applications: modeling the evacuation of high-rise buildings at the request of fire engineers and the flow of people in stadiums with the flagship example of the Allianz Arena in Munich as part of a European project.

Chapter 4 of the book is devoted to the issue of traffic modeling. First, I describe an introduction to traffic issues, then I present the Nagel-Schreckenberg model in its classic form. The following sections of the chapter show how the classic Na-Sch model can be adapted to urban conditions and the individual aspects of the model adapted to urban conditions are shown. The presented example concerns the flow of car traffic for the city of Krakow. Finally, examples of generated statistics for urban traffic, including, among others, fundamental diagrams, are presented.

Chapter 5 is devoted to the movement of skiers. This is a characteristic example in which the movement is continuous and the moving agents/skiers are strongly associated with the acting physical forces. In this case, it was decided to create a model that would operate on the principle of superposition of forces – this model is described in a continuous environment. The model takes into account the physical forces acting on the skier on the slope, and a special role is played by way-point forces, neighbor repulsion forces, or the proposed concept of social ellipses around the skier. Exemplary characteristics of skiers' movement were generated and discussed.

Chapter 6 is devoted to modeling the spread of oil on the surface of seas or oceans. In the first part of the chapter, this phenomenon is discussed from the theoretical side. Although there are oil spill spreading models based solely on Cellular Automata, a model that combines the Lagrangian discrete particle algorithm with the Cellular Automata approach was deliberately chosen. This significantly extends the possibilities of taking into account the components of processes accompanying oil spill modeling: advection, evaporation, emulsification, dissolution, dispersion, bio-degradation, sedimentation, and so on. Examples of the operation of the model for the Deep Water Horizon 2010 disaster are presented.

Chapter 7 summarizes the book. It discusses various collective aspects of the presented complex systems. Particular attention is paid to the phenomenon of emergence and self-organization. Reference is also made to Stephen Wolfram's thesis about the leading role of Cellular Automata as an effective tool for describing complex systems in the light of the work carried out and the various algorithms used.

Bibliography

[1] Sayama, H.: Introduction to the Modeling and Analysis of Complex Systems. Open SUNY, Geneseo, NY (2015)

[2] De Florio, V.: A Few Reflections on the Quality of Emergence in Complex Collective Systems, vol. 18, pp. 189–202. Springer, Berlin, Heidelberg (2017)

[3] Wyrzykowski, R. e.a. (ed.): Parallel Processing and Applied Mathematics, 8th International Conference, PPAM 2009, Wroclaw, Poland, September 13–16, 2009, Revised Selected Papers, Part II, *Lecture Notes in Computer Science*, vol. 6068. Springer (2010). https://doi.org/10.1007/978-3-642-14403-5

[4] Wąs, J.: Workshop on complex collective systems. http://www.ccs. agh.edu.pl/ (2022)

[5] Topa, P., Wąs, J.: Complex collective systems. J. Comput. Sci. **5**(5), 819–820 (2014). https://doi.org/10.1016/j.jocs.2014.08.001

[6] Topa, P., Wąs, J.: New trends in complex collective systems. J. Comput. Sci. **21**, 395–396 (2017). https://doi.org/10.1016/j.jocs.2017.05.020

[7] Wąs, J., Topa, P.: Special issue on complex collective systems. J. Comput. Sci. **32**, 68–69 (2019). https://doi.org/10.1016/j.jocs.2019.03.002

[8] Wolfram, S.: A New Kind of Science. Wolfram Media (2002). https://www.wolframscience.com

[9] Klüpfel, H.: Crowd Dynamics Phenomena, Methodology, and Simulation, chap. 10, pp. 213–243. Emerald (2009). https://doi.org/ 10.1108/9781848557512-010

[10] Burstedde, C., Klauck, K., Schadschneider, A., Zittartz, J.: Simulation of pedestrian dynamics using a two-dimensional cellular automaton. Phys. A: Stat. Mech. Appl. **295**(3–4), 507–525 (2001). https://doi.org/ 10.1016/S0378-4371(01)00141-8

[11] Was, J.: Cellular automata model of pedestrian dynamics for normal and evacuation conditions. In: 5th International Conference on Intelligent Systems Design and Applications (ISDA'05), pp. 154–159 (2005). https://doi.org/10.1109/ISDA.2005.31

[12] Wąs, J., Gudowski, B.: The application of cellular automata for pedestrian dynamic simulation. Automatyka 4173, 303–313 (2004)

[13] Wąs, J., Gudowski, B., Matuszyk, P.J.: Social distances model of pedestrian dynamics. In: S. El Yacoubi, B. Chopard, S. Bandini (eds.) Cellular Automata, pp. 492–501. Springer, Berlin, Heidelberg (2006)

[14] Wąs, J., Gudowski, B., Matuszyk, P.J.: New cellular automata model of pedestrian representation. In: S. El Yacoubi, B. Chopard, S. Bandini (eds.) Cellular Automata, pp. 724–727. Springer, Berlin, Heidelberg (2006)

[15] Dudek-Dyduch, E., Wąs, J.: Knowledge representation of pedestrian dynamics in crowd: Formalism of cellular automata. In: L. Rutkowski, R. Tadeusiewicz, L.A. Zadeh, J.M. Zurada (eds.) Artificial Intelligence and Soft Computing – ICAISC 2006, pp. 1101–1110. Springer, Berlin, Heidelberg (2006)

[16] Kułakowski, K., Wąs, J., Topa, P.: Simulation environment for modeling pedestrian dynamics. In: M.A. Kłopotek (ed.) Intelligent Information Systems: new approaches, pp. 251–252. Polish Academy of Science (2010)

[17] Wąs, J., Lubaś, R.: Adapting social distances model for mass evacuation simulation. Journal of Cellular Automata **8**(5/6), 395–405 (2013)

[18] Wąs, J., Lubaś, R.: Towards realistic and effective agent-based models of crowd dynamics. Neurocomputing **146**, 199–209 (2014). https://doi. org/10.1016/j.neucom.2014.04.057.   https://www.sciencedirect.com/ science/article/pii/S0925231214007838

[19] Wąs, J., Lubaś, R., Myśliwiec, W.: Proxemics in discrete simulation of evacuation. In: G.C. Sirakoulis, S. Bandini (eds.) Cellular Automata, pp. 768–775. Springer, Berlin, Heidelberg (2012)

[20] Porzycki, J., Lubaś, R., Mycek, M., Wąs, J.: Dynamic data–driven simulation of pedestrian movement with automatic validation. In: M. Chraibi, M. Boltes, A. Schadschneider, A. Seyfried (eds.) Traffic and Granular Flow '13, pp. 129–136. Springer International Publishing, Cham (2015)

[21] Lubaś, R., Wąs, J., Porzycki, J.: Cellular automata as the basis of effective and realistic agent-based models of crowd behavior. J. Supercomput. **72**, 2170–2196 (2016). https://doi.org/10.1007/s11227-016-1718-7

[22] Porzycki, J., Wąs, J., Hedayatifar, L., Hassanibesheli, F., Kułakowski, K.: Velocity correlations and spatial dependencies between neighbors in a unidirectional flow of pedestrians. Phys. Rev. E **96**, 022, 307 (2017). https://link.aps.org/doi/10.1103/PhysRevE.96.022307

[23] Porzycki, J., Schmidt-Polończyk, N., Wąs, J.: Pedestrian behavior during evacuation from road tunnel in smoke condition—empirical results. PLOS ONE **13**(8), 1–20 (2018). https://doi.org/10.1371/journal.pone.0201732

[24] Schmidt-Polończyk, N., Wąs, J., Porzycki, J.: What is the knowledge of evacuation procedures in road tunnels? survey results of users in Poland. Buildings **11**(4) (2021). https://doi.org/10.3390/buildings11040146. https://www.mdpi.com/2075-5309/11/4/146

[25] Bazior, G., Pałka, D., Wąs, J.: Cellular automata based modeling of competitive evacuation. In: G. Mauri, S. El Yacoubi, A. Dennunzio, K. Nishinari, L. Manzoni (eds.) Cellular Automata, pp. 451–459. Springer International Publishing, Cham (2018)

[26] Bazior, G., Pałka, D., Wąs, J.: Using cellular automata to model high density pedestrian dynamics. In: V.V. Krzhizhanovskaya, G. Závodszky, M.H. Lees, J.J. Dongarra, P.M.A. Sloot, S. Brissos, J. Teixeira (eds.) Computational Science – ICCS 2020, pp. 486–498. Springer International Publishing, Cham (2020)

[27] Holleczek, T., Tröster, G.: Particle-based model for skiing traffic. Phys. Rev. E **85**, 056, 101 (2012). https://link.aps.org/doi/10.1103/ PhysRevE.85.056101

[28] Korecki, T., Pałka, D., Wąs, J.: Adaptation of social force model for simulation of downhill skiing. Journal of Computational Science **16**, 29–42 (2016). https://doi.org/10.1016/j.jocs.2016.02.006. https://www.sciencedirect.com/science/article/pii/S1877750316300138

[29] Wąs, J., Bieliński, R., Gajewski, B., Orzechowski, P.: Issues of city traffic modeling based on cellular automata. Automatyka **13**, 1207–1217 (2009)

[30] Chmielewska, M., Kotlarz, M., Wąs, J.: Computer simulation of traffic flow based on cellular automata and multi-agent system. In: R. Wyrzykowski, E. Deelman, J. Dongarra, K. Karczewski, J. Kitowski, K. Wiatr (eds.) Parallel Processing and Applied Mathematics, pp. 517–527. Springer International Publishing, Cham (2016)

[31] Chmielewska, M., Wąs, J., Kotlarz, M.: Computer simulation of traffic flow based on cellular automata and multi-agent system. Presentation 4-th Workshop on Complex Collective Systems. Technical Report. AGH University of Science and Technology, Krakow (2015)

[32] Małecki, K., Kamiński, M., Wąs, J.: A multi-cell cellular automata model of traffic flow with emergency vehicles: Effect of a corridor of life and drivers' behaviour. J. Comput. Sci. **61**, 101, 628 (2022). https://doi.org/10.1016/j.jocs.2022.101628. https://www.sciencedirect.com/science/article/pii/S1877750322000515

[33] Szlachetka, M., Borkowski, D., Wąs, J.: The downselection of measurements used for free space determination in adas. J. Comput. Sci. **63**, 101, 762 (2022). https://doi.org/10.1016/j.jocs.2022.101762. https://www.sciencedirect.com/science/article/pii/S1877750322001454

[34] Szlachetka, M., Borkowski, D., Was, J.: Stationary environment models for advanced driver assistance systems. In: 2020 Signal Processing: Algorithms, Architectures, Arrangements, and Applications (SPA), pp. 116–121 (2020). https://doi.org/10.23919/SPA50552.2020.9241306

[35] Pikus, M., Wąs, J.: The application of virtual logic models to simulate real environment for testing advanced driving-assistance systems. In: 2019 24th International Conference on Methods and Models in Automation and Robotics (MMAR), pp. 544–547 (2019). https://doi.org/10.1109/MMAR.2019.8864634

[36] Service, N.O.: What is an oil seep? https://oceanservice.noaa.gov/facts/oilseep.html. Accessed: 2022-08-09

[37] Gług, M., Wąs, J.: Modeling of oil spill spreading disasters using combination of Langrangian discrete particle algorithm with cellular automata approach. Ocean Eng. **156**, 396–405 (2018). https://doi.org/10.1016/j.oceaneng.2018.01.029. https://www.sciencedirect.com/science/article/pii/S0029801818300295

2

Cellular Automata

The concept of a cellular automaton was proposed by the mathematician John von Neumann in the 1940s. von Neumann was working on a project to implement a self-replicating machine, i.e. creating a model of a self-steering machine that would duplicate its structure and transmit its features [1]. John von Neumann developed several projects of models of self-replicating automata, but the practical implementation of this project exceeded the capabilities of the then science and technology. This research, although not actually completed, has led to the emergence of a field of knowledge called Cellular Automata (CA), which occupies an important place in today's science and technology. An important figure in the preparation of the concept of Cellular Automata was also the mathematician Stanisław Ulam, who, while working on the growth of crystals, suggested to von Neumann the use of discrete space and discretized time in the cellular automaton formalism. So, we can say that each of these two researchers contributed one part to the formalism: von Neumann with his work on self-replication – "Automata", and Ulam with his work on discrete methods of observing crystals – "Cellular". In this way, a formalism was finally created that combines these two parts: Cellular Automata .

2.1 Definition of Cellular Automata

The cellular automaton, in the classic version, is defined with four parameters [2]: $(L, S, N,$ and $f)$,
where
   L – a lattice consisting of a set of regular cells,
   S – a set of cell states,
   N – a set of cell neighbors, and
   f – a transition function.

   The configuration $C_t : L \to S$ is a function that assigns each cell in the grid a certain state from a set of states. The f transition function changes the C_t configuration to the next C_{t+1} configuration. The configuration change equation is shown in the expression (2.1) along with the complementary equation (2.2).

$$C_{t+1}(r) = f(\{C_t(i)|i \in N(r)\}) \tag{2.1}$$

DOI: 10.1201/b23388-2

TABLE 2.1
Definition of Cellular Automata According to J. R. Weimar

Definition	Description
L	a lattice consists of cells(s)
$t \rightarrow t+1$	system evolves in discrete time steps
S	set of all cell states
$f : S^n \rightarrow S$	transition function definition respects the state of a given cell and states of neighboring cells
$N : \forall c \in N,$ $\forall r \in L : r + c \in L$	neighbor relation is local and identical

where

$N(r)$ – a set of neighbors of cell r
r – a current cell number
t – $t = t + 1$ discrete time step
i – a single cell

$$N(r) = \{i \in L | r - i \in N\} \tag{2.2}$$

Using the above designations and relationships, Table 2.1 presents the definition of a cellular automaton according to Jörg R. Weimar.

2.1.1   Elementary Cellular Automata

Probably the most famous publication on Cellular Automata is the over 1200-page work *A New Kind of Science* published in 2002 by Stephan Wolfram [3]. In the book, Wolfram describes a wide variety of classes of Cellular Automata, paying particular attention to the so-called ECA (Elementary Cellular Automata), also known as one-dimensional (1D) CA [4]:

Lattice – one-dimensional, represented as a line of cells.

States – binary states: 0 or 1.

Neighborhood – the cell (itself) and its two adjacent neighbors: right or left.

In a given time step, we have a set of cells with assigned states (0 or 1), which, depending on the adopted rules, evolve in subsequent time steps, taking the appropriate state values. The method of evaluation for an example configuration of cell states and a set of rules is shown in Figure 2.1. There is a transition function f, which calculates the state of a given cell in the current state on the basis of its state and two neighboring cells in the previous time step. Another important issue is the definition of boundary conditions. LuValle in [5] analyzes different influence types of boundary conditions, namely:

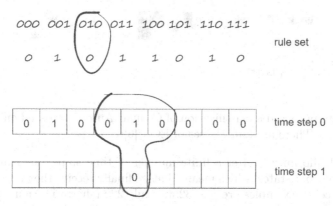

FIGURE 2.1
From a set of rules to Elementary Cellular Automata.

Periodic boundary conditions – we connect the first cell with the last one, creating a closed cycle (ring) – and then we have two neighbors for each cell – this is the most popular solution.

Random boundary conditions – we randomize the state values 0 or 1 for additional cells that are adjacent to the outermost cells.

Distributed boundary conditions – where the weights on the generation of a particular constant are equal to the weights of randomly selecting that constant from the list of the outputs of the rules [5].

Constant boundary conditions – where the boundary condition has a value of 0 or, alternatively, the boundary condition can have a constant value of 1.

Null boundary conditions – when in subsequent iterations (generations) edge cells that take on a null value are removed. In other words, the two edge cells are removed in each time step.

The solution that is most often used in practice is periodic boundary conditions

As an example, let's analyze the ECA of several adjacent cells for which we use the periodic boundary conditions scheme. For such a situation, the evolution of ECA can be described using a table taking into account the state of a cell and its left and right neighbors. So, when we consider the binary states for these three cells, we have $2 \times 2 \times 2 = 2^3 states$. One can point out $2^8 = 256$ ECA, indexed using an 8-bit binary number. Stephen Wolfram proposed a specific scheme of coding the 8-bit number applied in ECA: for instance, rule 30 can be denoted as follows: $rule15((00001111)_2 = 0 \times 2^7 + 0 \times 2^6 + 0 \times 2^5 + 0 \times 2^4 + 1 \times 2^3 + 1 \times 2^2 + 1 \times 2^1 + 1 \times 2^0 = 15)$ – the example is illustrated in Figure 2.2.

FIGURE 2.2
Elementary CA - rule 15

Wolfram proposed a classification of Cellular Automata based on observation of ECA. There are four classes of ECA [6]:

Class 1 – Uniformity – after a finite number of time steps, one can observe homogeneous states, which means that we finally receive the identical state for all cells. Examples are rule 32 and rule 222 (shown in Figure 2.3)

Class 2 – Repetition – after a finite number of time steps, one can observe repetitive (periodic patterns) or stable states. Examples are rule 108 and rule 190 (shown in Figure 2.4)

Class 3 – Random – one can observe chaotic structures (non-periodic patterns). Examples are rule 90 and rule 30 (shown in Figure 2.5). This rule is used as a simple pseudo-random number generator.

Class 4 – Complexity – one can observe repetitive oscillating patterns propagating locally in the lattice [4]. Examples are rule 54 and rule 110 (shown

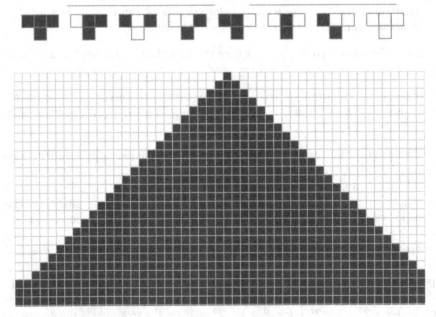

FIGURE 2.3
Example of class 1 of cellular automaton – rule 222 of ECA

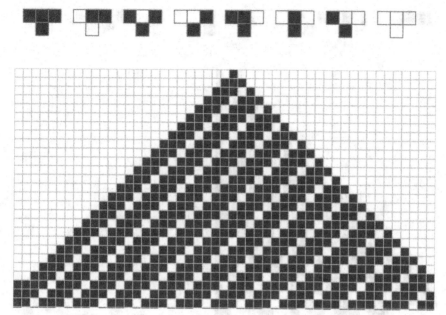

FIGURE 2.4
Example of class 2 of cellular automaton – rule 190 of ECA

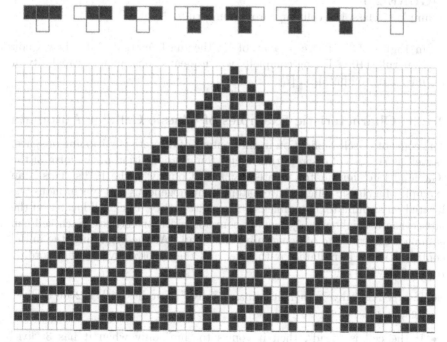

FIGURE 2.5
Example of class 3 of cellular automaton – rule 30 of ECA

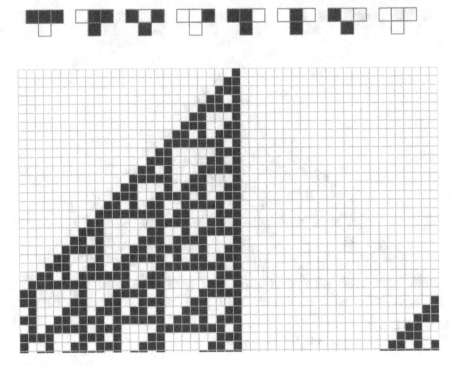

FIGURE 2.6
Example of class 4 of cellular automaton – rule 110 of ECA

in Figure 2.6). There is a proof by the mathematician Matthew Cook that rule 110 is Turing complete, which means consequently capability of universal computation [7].

2.1.2 Characteristic Examples of Classic Cellular Automata

The concept of self-replication in the context of discrete partitioning of space, as well as the use of discrete time steps, found application in the form of the "Game of Life" automaton created by John Conway in the 1970s. This is an example of a classic cellular automaton – a homogeneous and synchronous one located on an infinite, two-dimensional square lattice. Each cell located in the lattice has 8 neighbors adjacent by common sides or vertices. Each cell can assume a binary state of being "alive" or "dead". At the beginning, the initial configuration is formulated by the user and then evolves over time according to the following rules:

- If a cell is "alive", then it remains "alive" if it has either 2 or 3 "live" neighbors.

- If the cell is "dead", then it comes to "life" only when it has 3 "live" neighbors.

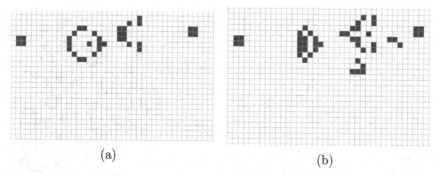

(a)　　　　　　　　　　　　　　　　(b)

FIGURE 2.7

On the left, the initial configuration of a Gosper Glider Gun – a characteristic configuration of Conway's Game of Life. On the right simulation after 27 steps – the first movable structure was formed a glider. (a) Gosper Glider Gun – step 0. (b) Gosper Glider Gun – step 27.

Two-dimensional Cellular Automata in the Game of Life, despite the simplicity of the rules, can create very complex structures. An example is the Gosper Glider Gun, which generates a moving structure called a glider every few cycles. Figure 2.7 shows a structure discovered by Bill Gosper of the University of Berkeley, named after its creator – the Gosper Glider Gun. As a result of the simulation, cyclically moving gliders are generated that move down the grid, Figure 2.8.

An example of another very popular cellular automaton is Langton's Ant [8]. It was defined by Chris G. Langton in 1986. A cell called an ant is

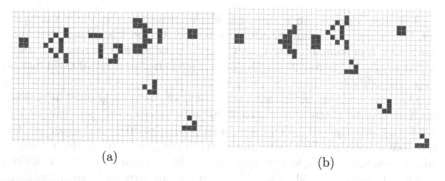

(a)　　　　　　　　　　　　　　　　(b)

FIGURE 2.8

On the left simulation of a Gosper Glider Gun. Two movable structures gliders are visible. On the right, cyclically generated structures, gliders, are visible. (a) Gosper Glider Gun – step 71. (b) Gosper Glider Gun – step 91.

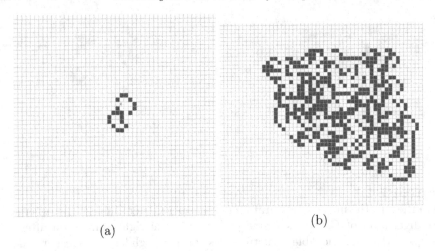

(a)   (b)

FIGURE 2.9
On the left – initial phase of Langton's Ant walking – the initial phase of
chaotic wandering. On the right – simulation after 7000 steps – visible characteristic traces in the phase of chaotic wandering. (a) Langton's Ant – step
100. (b) Lanton's Ant – step 7000.

placed on an infinite square board. The ant behaves according to the following
rules:

- If the ant is on a white field, it rotates to the right (right angle), changes
  the color of the field to black, and moves to the next cell;

- If the ant is on a black field, it rotates to the left (right angle), changes
  the color of the field to white, and moves to the next cell.

The ant is placed on a square grid. According to the above rules, the
ant first starts wandering around the lattice. In the first phase, the ant's
movement area is small, however gradually expanding, and no regular pattern
is discernible. In Figure 2.9, patterns are placed after 100 and 7000 simulation
steps, respectively.

Over the next several thousand iterations, we observe a gradual increase in
the area covered by the ant. Up to about 10000 steps, clear patterns are still
not found. After about 10000 steps, a surprising simulation is observed, the
ant stops wandering chaotically, and starts to create a spatial pattern – simple
and increasingly longer, several cells wide – this pattern is called a highway.

Over the next several thousand iterations, the structure called the highway is consistently expanded (Figure 2.10). All the time it remains in the
shape of a straight, i.e., non-curved structure, and in subsequent iterations, it
tends to infinity or to the previously defined limits of the cellular automaton
grid. The simulation of Langton's Ant after 20000 iterations is presented in
Figure 2.11.

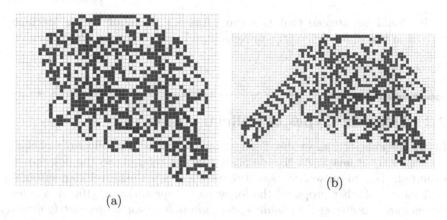

(b)

(a)

FIGURE 2.10
On the left – visible maximum growth of the structure in the phase of chaotic wandering. On the right – a surprising change in the resulting structure created, after about 10000 steps of chaotic wandering, a regular structure called highway begins to be created. (a) Langton's Ant – step 10000. (b) Langton's Ant – step 11000.

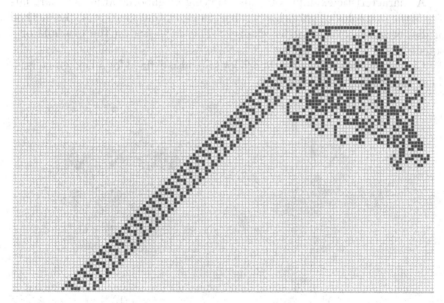

FIGURE 2.11
Langton's Ant – step 20000 – the constantly expanding highway structure is visible.

It should be stressed that Langton's Ant is a universal Turing Machine defined in two dimensions – the universality of this automaton was presented in [9].

2.2 Different Types of Cellular Automata

In the previous section, we discussed examples of flagship applications of classic Cellular Automata. At this point, it is worth referring to the descriptive definition: i.e., to answer the question of what is a classic cellular automaton? Jacques Ferber proposed the following interpretation in [10]: *A cellular automaton is a discrete, dynamic system whose behavior is completely determined by the conditions of local relations.* Alberto Dennuzio, Enrico Formanti, and Julien Provillard in [11] claim that "a cellular automaton is made of identical finite automata arranged on a regular lattice. Each automaton updates its state by a local rule on the basis of its state and the one of a fixed set of neighbors." Thus, a classic cellular automaton is homogeneous, synchronous, and deterministic. Regarding a square lattice, one can point out two basic kinds of neighborhood applied in 2D CA as presented in Figure 2.12, namely von Neumann neighborhood with four neighbors and the Moore neighborhood with eight neighbors.

A characteristic example of a time-varying neighborhood for a square lattice is the Margolus neighborhood. Then, in individual time steps, the method of discretization of the lattice changes. This is shown on the example of a square lattice in Figure 2.13.

Characteristic types of neighborhoods are also defined for a hexagonal grid. They are shown in Figure 2.14.

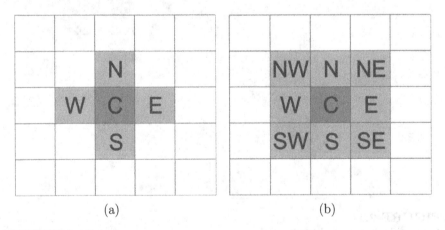

(a) (b)

FIGURE 2.12
Two popular neighborhoods defined for 2D Cellular Automata with a square lattice. (a) von Neumann neighborhood. (b) Moore neighborhood.

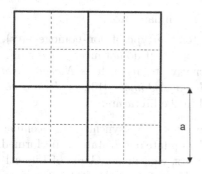 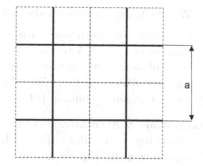

Margolus neighbourhood phase 1   Margolus neighbourhood phase 2

FIGURE 2.13
Two consecutive phases of Margolus neighborhood defined for 2D Cellular
Automata with a square lattice.

It should be emphasized that any new neighborhood schemes are created
using tessellation methods, such as Voronoi tessellation [12].

It is worth looking at the basic classifications of Cellular Automata:

Homogeneous vs. Non-homogeneous Cellular Automata. The definition of a
  homogeneous cellular automaton is not a problem: we have a defined grid
  of cells that assumes a state from a defined set of states, and the same
  transition rule applies to the entire lattice. In a situation where:

  • transition rules may be different for different cells,
  • different types of cells can assume different states, and
  • the lattice of a cellular automaton can change over time.

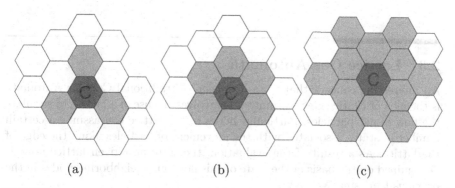

(a)   (b)   (c)

FIGURE 2.14
Hexagonal lattice with three characteristic types of neighborhood. (a) Tripod
neighborhood scheme. (b) Honey neighborhood scheme. (c) Hexagonal star
neighborhood scheme.

We are dealing with a non-homogeneous cellular automaton.

Depending on the nomenclature used (or the type of non-homogeneity), there are various CA terms in the literature that do not meet the assumptions of non-homogeneity. Thus, alternative terms such as *Non-uniform Cellular Automata* [11], *Irregular Cellular Automata* [13], or *Inhomogeneous Cellular Automata* [14] are used in the literature.

Synchronous vs Asynchronous Cellular Automata: A synchronous cellular automaton is an automaton in which the update of cell states is performed simultaneously [15]. Such a scheme occurs, e.g., in the Game of Life cellular automaton, where using simple rules based on the state of a given cell and neighboring cells, we determine the state of the entire lattice. In a situation where the synchronization of cell states takes place in a specific order (e.g., in a user-defined or randomly determined order), then we are dealing with an asynchronous automaton [16]. In Asynchronous Cellular Automata, we can deal with two different update schemes :

- Time-driven – the update takes place using the built-in clock with a time variable
- Step-driven – the update is carried out using a queuing algorithm: predefined, randomly generated sequence for the whole simulation or each time step [12]

Deterministic vs Probabilistic Cellular Automata: Cellular Automata rules can be deterministic, where each new configuration is defined by deterministic rules. Another possibility is to use probabilistic rules. In the simulation of complex systems, the use of probabilistic rules gives many new possibilities. In the simulation of complex systems, the use of probabilistic rules allows, in the vast majority of cases, realism to be increased.

2.3 Lattice Gas Automata

An interesting concept that is an extension of traditional Cellular Automata is the idea of Lattice Gas Automata. It involves the use of a lattice to simulate the flow of gas particles. Particular nodes of the lattice can assume a certain number of states associated with the movement of particles along the edge of the lattice. As a result of the evaluation, the state in a given lattice node is determined on the basis of the state of this node and neighboring nodes in the previous time step.

It should be emphasized that the states of particles migrating between nodes are given as Boolean values, i.e., the presence of a gas particle or the absence of a particle (the concept of particles' "fuzziness" is not assumed). Gas particles can move along the lattice (grid) lines or collide with other particles.

Collision rules are created for each of the grid gas methods, which occur when two or more particles arrive at the same node from different directions. The principles of mass and momentum conservation are assumed.

The first method of this type was proposed in the years 1973–76 based on a square grid proposed by Jean Hardy, Yves Pomeau, and Olivier de Pazzis. The gas particles moved along the edges of the grid, while the collision occurred – when the particles met in the up-down (vertical) system, then after the collision, they moved in the right-left (horizontal) system. Similarly, after a collision of particles in the right-left (horizontal) system, the particles were redirected to the up-down (vertical) system. This method was named HPP after its three creators. Its significant advantage is its simplicity, while its disadvantage is anisotropy. The model is therefore deterministic, due to the lack of rules related to random variables.

To avoid the disadvantages of anisotropy, in the 1980s, three other researchers, Uriel Frisch, Brosl Hasslacher, and Yves Pomeau, proposed a method based on a hexagonal grid. This method was also named after its creators and is now known as FHP. The main change compared to the previous method is that particles that are centered on each other from two directions toward the center of the hexagon are directed according to randomization (random variable) in one of the two possible directions. The model is therefore probabilistic.

The diagrams of particle collisions for the HPP and FHP models are presented in Figure 2.15

Another important method, which is an extension of Lattice Gas Automata (HPP and FHP methods), is the Lattice Boltzmann method. In the Lattice

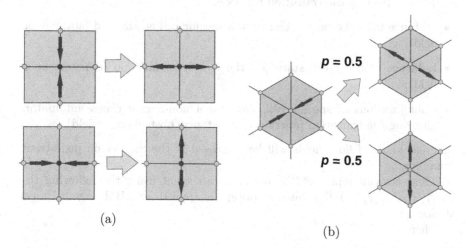

(a)

(b)

FIGURE 2.15

Characteristics of the HPP and FHP methods. (a) Collision scheme for the HPP model. (b) Collision scheme for the FHP model.

Boltzmann algorithm, binary representation of moving particles has been replaced with a particle distribution function. The function points out the position of the particle on the lattice (with some probability) in time and with a specific velocity. Calculations are made using the Lattice Boltzmann equation [17]. This method, additionally, uses a collision operator instead of a set of collision rules (relatively simple) used in HPP or FHP. Currently, Lattice Boltzmann is one of the most popular methods belonging to the Computational Fluid Dynamics (CFD) family.

2.4   Extensions of the Concept of Cellular Automata

In order to simulate complex systems, one goes beyond the classic definition of CA discussed at the beginning of this chapter. Frequently used methods are the previously discussed Asynchronous Automata or Non-homogeneous Automata.

We can assume that a certain state of the cell corresponds to the entity that we place on the lattice. In the simplest case, this will be the cell occupancy state, which represents a particle, pedestrian, skier, or vehicle. It moves on the grid according to the transition rules.

A simple procedure that modifies the transition function of the Cellular Automata is the use of additional layers to the Cellular Automata lattice (occupancy lattice – occupied by particular entities). Such layers can be additional lattices with so-called floor fields, which take into account additional conditions affecting the transition function:

- Distance from the target, i.e., from a specific cell on the grid (static floor field);

- Influence of other cell states on the transition function (dynamic floor field);

- Configurations of specific cell states in a non-homogeneous automaton affecting the transition function (for instance, obstacle floor field).

Different kinds of floor fields will be discussed in the chapter on pedestrian dynamics.

Thus, we can represent the entity as an agent using the following tuple $A_j = (\tau_j, (x_j, y_j), R_j)$. Such a concept is applied for ABM (Agent-Based Modeling),

where

τ_j – type of agent j,

x_j, y_j – coordinates of agent j,

R_j – strategic, tactical, and operational ability of agent j.

I have described the problem of connecting Cellular Automata with the agent system in more detail in [21]. In this way, complex rules can be created that combine a cellular automaton with Agent-Based Modeling [19]. Examples will be described in the following sections.

Bibliography

[1] von Neumann, J.: Theory of Self-Reproducing Automata. University of Illinois Press, Champaign, IL (1966)

[2] Weimar, J.: Simulation with Cellular Automata. Logos–Verlag, Champaign, IL (1998)

[3] Wolfram, S.: A New Kind of Science. Wolfram Media (2002). https://www.wolframscience.com

[4] Berto, F., Tagliabue, J.: Cellular Automata. In: E.N. Zalta (ed.) The Stanford Encyclopedia of Philosophy, Spring 2022 edn. Metaphysics Research Lab, Stanford University, Champaign, IL (2022)

[5] LuValle, B.: The effects of boundary conditions on cellular automata. Complex Systems **28**, 97–124 (2019). https://doi.org/10.25088/ComplexSystems.28.1.97

[6] Shiffman, D., Fry, S., Marsh, Z.: The Nature of Code. D. Shiffman (2012). https://books.google.pl/books?id=hoK6lgEACAAJ

[7] Cook, M.: Universality in elementary cellular automata. Complex Syst. **15**, 120–149 (2004)

[8] Langton, C.G.: Studying artificial life with cellular automata. Physica D: Nonlinear Phenomena **22**(1), 120–149 (1986). https://doi.org/10.1016/0167-2789(86)90237-X. https://www.sciencedirect.com/science/article/pii/016727898690237X. Proceedings of the Fifth Annual International Conference

[9] Gajardo, A., Moreira, A., Goles, E.: Complexity of Langton's Ant. Discret. Appl. Math. **117**(1), 41–50 (2002). https://doi.org/10.1016/S0166-218X(00)00334-6. https://www.sciencedirect.com/science/article/pii/S0166218X00003346

[10] Ferber, J.: Multi-Agent Systems: An Introduction to Distributed Artificial Intelligence, 1st edn. Addison-Wesley Longman Publishing Co., Inc., Boston, MA (1999)

[11] Dennunzio, A., Formenti, E., Provillard, J.: Non-uniform cellular automata: Classes, dynamics, and decidability. Inf. Comput. **215**, 32–46 (2012). https://doi.org/10.1016/j.ic.2012.02.008. https://www.sciencedirect.com/science/article/pii/S0890540112000685

[12] Topa, P.: Cellular automata as an efficient and flexible computational framework for modeling and simulation of realworld, multiscale complex systems. Publishing House of AGH University (2019). https://winntbg.bg.agh.edu.pl/skrypty4/0616/cellular.pdf

[13] Bochenek, B., Tajs-Zielińska, K.: Gotica – generation of optimal topologies by irregular cellular automata. Struct. Multidiscipl. Optim. **55**, 1–13 (2017). https://doi.org/10.1007/s00158-016-1614-z

[14] Hartman, H., Vichniac, G.Y.: Inhomogeneous cellular automata (inca). In: E. Bienenstock, F.F. Soulié, G. Weisbuch (eds.) Disordered Systems and Biological Organization, pp. 53–57. Springer, Berlin, Heidelberg (1986)

[15] Fatès, N.: A guided tour of asynchronous cellular automata (2014). https://doi.org/10.48550/ARXIV.1406.0792. https://arxiv.org/abs/1406.0792

[16] Schönfisch, B., de Roos, A.: Synchronous and asynchronous updating in cellular automata. Biosystems **51**(3), 123–143 (1999). https://doi.org/10.1016/S0303-2647(99)00025-8. https://www.sciencedirect.com/science/article/pii/S0303264799000258

[17] Wolf-Gladrow, D.A.: Lattice Gas Cellular Automata and Lattice Boltzmann Models. Springer, Berlin (2000)

[18] Lubaś, R., Wąs, J., Porzycki, J.: Cellular automata as the basis of effective and realistic agent-based models of crowd behavior. J. Supercomput. **72**, 2170–2196 (2016). https://doi.org/10.1007/s11227-016-1718-7

[19] Bandini, S., Manzoni, S., Vizzari, G.: Situated cellular agents: a model to simulate crowding dynamics. Trans. Inf. **E87D**(3), 669–676 (2004)

3

Crowd Dynamics and Behavior

3.1 Basics of Modeling of Crowd Dynamics and Behavior

Modeling the dynamics and behavior of pedestrians is a characteristic example of a complex system where collective behavior plays a large role. Individual people can have different goals, so the range of behavior is wide: from neutrality, through cooperation of people in the crowd, to mutual competition. As a result of the analysis of particular pedestrians behaviors, we get a fascinating picture of the whole crowd, emerging from the behavior of individual individuals or groups.

The behavior of crowd has fascinated people since ancient times and the phenomenon of the crowd is described in many ancient literary works – for example in the Bible. The ancient Greeks distinguished between different terms for crowd, two of which appear to be the most important: the Greek word *plethos* – the entire body of citizens, and the Greek word *ochlos* - for anonymous crowd/mob [1]. The term *plethos* refers to a personally understood large group of people, while the term *ochlos* refers to an anonymously understood crowd of people. Following the term *crowd*, the famous Roman orator, politician, and philosopher Marcus Tullius Cicero delivered a well-known sentence: "Senatores boni viri, senatus autem mala bestia", which can be translated from Latin as "Senators are good men, whilst the senate is an evil beast". This means that in certain external circumstances, the behavior of individuals follows predictable rules, and the end result of the behavior of the entire group may be surprising and even dangerous. One of the first studies on the phenomenon of the Crowd was published by Gustave Le Bon, in which he reflects on the "mind of the collective" [2]. Crowd can be classified in many ways. One of the most popular classifications is proposed by Forsyth [3]. According to Forsyth, a crowd can be classified as follows (Figure 3.1).

Various crowd models can be created based on theory, observations, and real-world data. From an individual point of view, a human in a crowd can be considered an agent who has abilities or knowledge at various levels. In reference to Adam Newell's notion of knowledge levels of artificial agents, one can distinguish different levels of the pedestrian decision-making process including social, rational, cognitive, reactive, and physical levels. Often, in practice, a simplified version of the decision-making levels is used, which

DOI: 10.1201/b23388-3

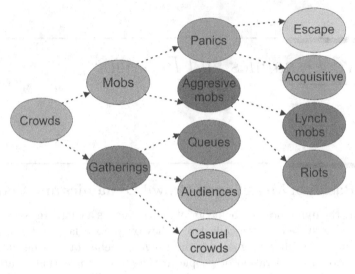

FIGURE 3.1
Types of crowd – according to Forsyth [3].

comes down to a three-level scheme: strategic, tactical, and operational levels
(Figure 3.2).

One can point out different approaches in crowd dynamics modeling, depending on the scale of the constructed model. The microscopic models take
into account the behavior of individuals/people and, on the basis of the ac-
tions of individual units, the overall image of the crowd is formed (Figure 3.3).
There is also a mesoscopic approach in which we consider groups of pedestrians, i.e., individuals are aggregated into groups and we consider the impact
of individual groups [4]. In the macroscopic approach, we treat the crowd

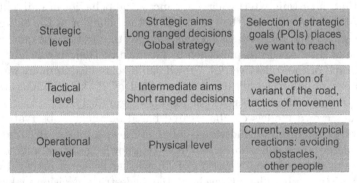

FIGURE 3.2
Decision-making by pedestrians represented by agents.

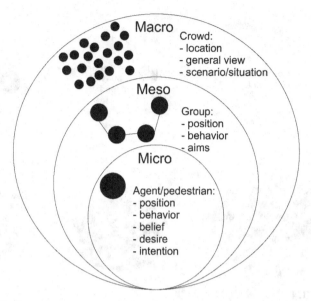

FIGURE 3.3
Scales in pedestrians modeling including micro-scale – particular pedestrians/agents, meso-scale – groups of pedestrians, and macro-scale – the whole crowd.

analogously to a flowing liquid, i.e., we represent its flow using appropriate physical equations.

The issues related to crowd density are important in crowd modeling. In modeling pedestrian traffic or modeling evacuation, there is so-called level of services – where different crowd density ranges are assumed (Figure 3.4).

3.1.1 Macroscopic Approach

Macroscopic models are focused on complex crowd behavior and dynamics, where the overall crowd image can be described by appropriate flow equations [5], as an analogy to gas or liquid flow. Numerous macroscopic models of crowds are known in the literature [6], [7], [8], etc. Helbing proposed in [6] a fluid dynamics approach, namely gas kinetic equations, in order to model crowds of pedestrians. Helbing's work is based on previous work by Henderson, but in contrast to this work, it is assumed that the conservation of momentum and energy does not hold. In this model, pedestrians are aggregated into groups with a specific type of motion μ with different assigned directions of motion. Pedestrians from the particular group μ at time t are characterized by the pedestrian's location $\overrightarrow{x}$, velocity $\overrightarrow{v}_\mu$, and intended velocity $\overrightarrow{v}_\mu$. Finally, in the specific area A, we consider the density of pedestrians $\widehat{\rho}_\mu(\overrightarrow{x}, \overrightarrow{v}_\mu, \overrightarrow{v}_0^\mu)$ and we are able to establish equations of motion. Thanks to that, it is possible to

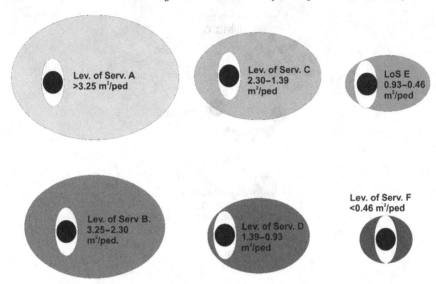

FIGURE 3.4
Six basic levels of services taking into account available space for a single
pedestrian in a considered scenario according to John J. Fruin [9].

calculate: $\langle \rho_\mu \rangle$ – pedestrians' spatial density, $\overrightarrow{v}_\mu$ – pedestrians' mean velocity,
and $\langle (\delta v_{\mu,i})^2 \rangle$ – velocity variance. $\mathcal{N}_\mu$ is the number of pedestrians (type μ)
located in area $A = A(\overrightarrow{x})$ in $\overrightarrow{x}$ having the approximate intended velocity $\overrightarrow{v}_0^\mu$
using actual velocity $\overrightarrow{v}_\mu$.

Thus, one can define the following equation, Eq. 3.1:

$$\widehat{\rho}_\mu(\overrightarrow{x}, \overrightarrow{v}_\mu, \overrightarrow{v}_\mu^0, t) \equiv \widehat{\rho}_\mu(\overrightarrow{x}, \overrightarrow{u}_\mu, t) := \frac{\mathcal{N}_\mu(\mathcal{U}(\overrightarrow{x}) \times \mathcal{V}(\overrightarrow{u}_\mu), t)}{A \cdot V} \tag{3.1}$$

The notation $\mathcal{U}(\overrightarrow{x})$ means a neighborhood around $\overrightarrow{x}$ with all accessible
places, Eq. 3.2. It belongs to domain $\mathcal{M}$, which constitutes a *Movement area*
for pedestrians.

$$\mathcal{U}(\overrightarrow{x}) := \{\overrightarrow{x}^* \in \mathcal{M} : \| \overrightarrow{x}^* - \overrightarrow{x} \|_l \le r\} \tag{3.2}$$

Analogically, $\mathcal{V}(\overrightarrow{u}_\mu)$ means a neighborhood of $\overrightarrow{u}_\mu := (\overrightarrow{u}_\mu, \overrightarrow{v}_\mu^0)$ taking
into account volume $V = V(\overrightarrow{u}_\mu)$.

Thanks to the previous steps, continuity equations can be formulated,
Eq. 3.3, which is characteristic for gas-kinetic approaches. In this equation,
m_μ means the average mass of pedestrians of type μ, the forces are often of
secondary importance and can be neglected $\overrightarrow{f}_\mu := m_\mu \overrightarrow{v}_\mu$, relaxation time
$\tau_\mu \equiv \frac{m_\mu}{\gamma_\mu}$, and finally we can take into account four effects in pedestrians'
movement: the tendency to reach intended velocity $\overrightarrow{v}_\mu$, bilateral interactions
between pedestrians $\widehat{S}_{\mu\nu}$, change of pedestrian's POI (Point of Interest) described in the equations as a change in pedestrian type from μ to ν, and finally,

change in density $\widehat{\rho}_\mu(\overrightarrow{x}, \overrightarrow{v'}_\mu, \overrightarrow{v'}^0_\mu, t)$ based on changes in pedestrians' numbers entering or leaving a given *Movement area* in a time unit.

$$\frac{d\widehat{\rho}_\mu}{dt} \equiv$$

$$\frac{\partial\widehat{\rho}_\mu}{\partial t} + \nabla_{\overrightarrow{x}}(\widehat{\rho}_\mu, \overrightarrow{v'}_\mu) + \nabla_{\overrightarrow{v'}_\mu}\left(\widehat{\rho}_\mu \frac{\overrightarrow{f_\mu}}{m_\mu}\right) + \nabla_{\overrightarrow{v'}^0_\mu}(\widehat{\rho}_\mu, \overrightarrow{v'}^0_\mu) :=$$

$$\frac{\widehat{\rho}^0_\mu - \widehat{\rho}_\mu}{\tau_\mu} + \sum_\nu \hat{S}_{\mu\nu} + \sum_\nu \hat{C}_{\mu\nu} + \widehat{q}_\mu. \qquad (3.3)$$

Next, on the basis of change of two types of pedestrians (two states μ to ν), we are able to formulate hydrodynamic equations taking into account: *mass density, momentum density*, and finally, *energy density*.

The advantages of this approach are good physical foundations, the ability to define crowd streams, or propagation of a density wave. Unfortunately, macroscopic models are difficult to expand and use; adding new states, goals, or model parameters is sometimes difficult and often too costly from the numerical point of view.

3.1.2 Microscopic Approach

The microscopic approach in crowd dynamics takes into account positions, behavior, basic rules, and/or more sophisticated individual properties of pedestrians, such as beliefs, desire, and intentions in the BDI agent model [10].

If we assume that a pedestrian represents skills at the operational level and the tactical level (i.e., the simulation implements simple predefined scenarios), then we are dealing with a cellular automaton system, a queuing system, or a simple case of molecular dynamic-based systems. Taking into account the terminology of agent systems, in these simple scenarios we deal with reactive agents. If we add a strategic level to the operational and tactical skills of an agent, regarding the definition of goals, then we deal with agent-based models (which can be represented by cognitive agents). In a pedestrian's decision-making, one can point out different levels of abstraction and knowledge levels according to Allen Newell's approach [11]:

- cognitive

- social

- rational

- reactive

- physical

3.2   Molecular Dynamics-Based Approach

The most famous example of a model based on molecular dynamics is a model created by Helbing, Molnar, Farkas, and Vicsek [12], known as the *Social Force Model*. They proved in the article that pedestrian dynamics can be described using one way for normal as well as for evacuation or panic situations [13]. In the Social Force Model for normal situations, one can point out five main components: *Acceleration* responsible for adaptation of the current velocity vector into calculation of desired velocity vector on the basis of current velocity vector, *Repulsion (Social) Force* $f_{ij}^{soc}(t)$ which takes into account proxemic effects among pedestrians (social distancing, etc.), *Attractive (Social) Force* $f_{ij}^{att}(t)$ which takes into account the groups' cohesion effect, *Boundary Force* $f_{ib}(t)$ which shows interaction with boundaries, and the *POI Attractive Force (toward Point of Interest)* $f_{ik}^{att}(t)$ with forces that originate from the POI, which attract pedestrians (Figure 3.5).

In order to mimic pedestrian dynamics in panic situations (or competitive or non-competitive evacuation), we should include an additional force, namely the *Physical Interaction Force* $f_{ib}^{ph}(t)$, which takes into account possible physical contact between pedestrians. In this context, we should take into account

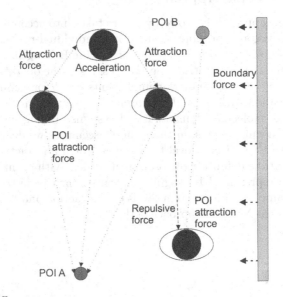

FIGURE 3.5
Mechanism of superposition of forces in the Social Force Model. Group of pedestrians head toward POI A (Point of Interest A), while a pedestrian heads toward POI B (Point of Interest B). The figure shows the main types of forces acting in the system for a normal situation.

Body Force with a counteracting effect for particular neighboring pedestrians, and additionally *Sliding Friction Force*, as well as a physical interaction force with boundaries. Similar forces have been used in popular extensions of the Social Force Model [14] or [15].

In the Helbing-Molnár-Farkas-Vicsek (HMFV) model [12], the pedestrians' motion can be denoted using the following equation (Eq. 3.4):

$$f_i(t) = f_i^{acc}(t) + \sum_{j(\neq i)} (f_{ij}^{soc}(t) + f_{ij}^{att}(t) + f_{ij}^{ph}) + \sum_b f_{ib}(t) + \sum_k f_{ik}^{att}(t). \quad (3.4)$$

In this context, $f_i^{acc}(t)$ is described as the acceleration term. In our model created with Tytko, Mamica, and PąŹkala [13], it is described using the following term (Eq 3.5):

$$f_i^{acc}(t) = \frac{v_i^0(t)e_i^0(t) - v_i(t)}{\tau_i} m_i \quad (3.5)$$

where $v_i(t)$ represents the actual velocity, $v_i^0(t)$ represents desired speed, and $e_i^0(t)$ denotes direction with the usage of the relaxation time τ_i.

Next $f_{ij}^{soc}(t)$ describes a repulsive social force [12]. It can be formulated as Eq. 3.6:

$$f_{ij}^{soc}(t) = A_i exp \left(\frac{r_{ij} - d_{ij}}{B_i} \right) n_{ij} \left(\lambda_i + (1 - \lambda_i) \frac{1 + cos(\varphi_{ij})}{2} \right) \quad (3.6)$$

Interaction strength is denoted as A_i, while the range of the repulsive interactions is denoted as B_i. Pedestrians i and j are located in a certain distance d_{ij}. The symbol r_{ij} describes the sum of particular radius r_i and r_j. Next, n_{ij} denotes a normalized vector defined from pedestrian j to i. Finally, φ_{ij} describes an angle between $e_i^0(t)$ and n_{ij}.

The symbol $f_{ij}^{att}(t)$ represents the attractive social force among people (namely groups or families) while, $f_{ik}^{att}(t)$ is the POI attractive force (acting toward POIs).

For evacuation or a panic scenario, we can introduce physical interaction forces f_{ij}^{ph} responsible for the interaction between particular pedestrians and their neighbors. The forces are initialized when pedestrians will be very close to each other, especially when there is physical contact between them. In practice, it forces the direction of movement due to physical constraints. These forces can be described as follows on the basis of [12], [16]:

$$f_{ij}^{ph} = f_{ij}^{body} + f_{ij}^{friction} \quad (3.7)$$

f_{ij}^{body} denotes the body force responsible for counteracting compression.

$$f_{ij}^{body} = kg(r_{ij} - d_{ij})n_{ij} \quad (3.8)$$

$f_{ij}^{friction}$ denotes interactions among bodies connected with physical effects of friction.

$$f_{ij}^{friction} = \kappa g(r_{ij} - d_{ij})\Delta v_{ji}^t t_{ij} \quad (3.9)$$

In this equation, k and κ are constants, while $g(x)$ is the function that returns x, if $x \geq 0$, otherwise 0. Next $t_{ij} = (-n_{ij}^2, n_{ij}^1)$ is a tangential direction to n_{ij} and tangential velocity difference is denoted as $\Delta v_{ji}^t = (v_j - v_i) \cdot t_{ij}$.

The interaction with walls and other obstacles is treated analogously [14]:

$$f_{ib}(t) = f_{ib}^{body} + f_{ib}^{friction} \tag{3.10}$$

3.3   Cellular Automata-Based Approach

As mentioned in the previous chapter, a cellular automaton can be defined as the quadruple (L, S, f, N), where L is a lattice composed of cells [17], each cell from lattice L defined using coordinates (x_0, y_0) located in lattice L with the available set of states S evolves according to the transition function $f : S^n \to S$ and the neighborhood relations are local and uniform.

In Cellular Automata-based models, we understand the flow of pedestrians as a spatially distributed process of particular pedestrians allocated as states of the lattice. The space of the model where the pedestrians are located is usually represented as a 2D lattice $40\ cm \times 40\ cm$ or $50\ cm \times 50\ cm$, which corresponds to the projection from above of a pedestrian on a horizontal surface. $C_t : L \to S$ configuration denotes a function which connects the state with each cell $c\{x, y\} \in L$. The next configuration C_{t+1} is derived from C_t using the transition function f (Eq. 3.11)

$$C_{t+1}(r) = f(\{C_t(i) \mid i \in N(r)\}) \tag{3.11}$$

where $N(r)$ means a set of neighbors of a cell r and $N(r) = \{i \in L | r - i \in N\}$).

The central cell with a pedestrian is denoted using the coordinates (x_0, y_0), and in such a case, the von Neumann neighborhood is defined by Eq. 3.12:

$$N_{(x_0, y_0)} = \{(x, y) : |x - x_0| + |y - y_0| \leqslant R\} \tag{3.12}$$

while the Moore neighborhood 3.13 of the central cell denoted as (x_0, y_0) (with eight neighbors) is defined as:

$$N_{(x_0, y_0)} = \{(x, y) : |x - x_0| \leqslant R, |y - y_0| \leqslant R\} \tag{3.13}$$

In Figure 3.6, one can observe the matrix of probability of preferred walking directions for the two most popular neighborhoods, namely the von Neumann neighborhood and Moore neighborhood.

The most relevant neighborhood is Moore's neighborhood because of the greater precision in mapping the motion. The probability of entering a cell in the Moore scheme can be denoted as: $\sum_{i=-1, j=-1}^{i=1, j=1} M_{i,j} = 1$ Additional grids are also used in the transition function, called dynamic fields, which

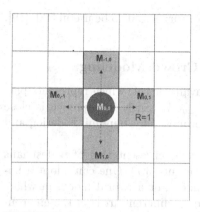 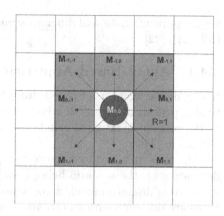

FIGURE 3.6

Transition matrix for Cellular Automata-based models of crowds for a neighborhood with the radius $R = 1$. On the left, the von Neumann neighborhood, on the right, the Moore neighborhood.

modify the transition function and direct the movement of people depending on various factors: Static floor field – distance from the target, dynamic floor field – dynamics of flow of other people, and proxemic floor field – keeping the distance from a pedestrian. Some examples of floor field are presented in Eq. 3.7.

3.4 Discrete Agent-Based Models of Crowd Dynamics

A great need for effective and efficient crowd dynamics models can be observed. Macroscopic models enable the modeling of large areas with pedestrians, give a certain picture of the crowd flow, but do not allow for a detailed analysis of crowd dynamics and behavior.

Microscopic models based on molecular dynamics allow for precise calculation of physical quantities: such as local pressure in a crowd, acting forces, or velocity correlations. They do not cause large discretization errors. Unfortunately, they are computationally expensive (the problem of N-body simulation) and, when simulating large areas, there are performance issues. In many national and international projects in which I have participated, a scenario was repeated in which the method based on molecular dynamics was perfect for calculating forces, pressures, or pedestrian crossing times for a small area, but it was unsuitable for the implementation of complex scenarios in larger areas.

The modeling methodology based on CA and ABM (Agent-Based Modeling), which I have developed with various colleagues in several versions for the implementation of different scenarios, turned out to be useful [18], [19], [20], [21], [22].

3.4.1 Agent-Based Approach in Crowd Modeling

Let us define agent a_i of type τ from the available set, which represents particular pedestrians $a_i \in A$, where $A = \bigcup_{\tau \in T} A_\tau$. Such an approach is close to the concept of situated cellular agents proposed by Bandini, Federici, and Vizzari in [23].

The first step is to configure the physical representation of pedestrians depending on the scenario being handled (Figure 3.7). One can adopt a homogeneous discrete model, a continuous model, or a hybrid model in which there are different representations of agents in different areas of the environment. Figure 3.8 shows examples of popular representations of humans in 2D space, which we use in our models.

Physical representation of the environment: The physical representation of the environment is created on the basis of Geographic Information System (GIS) maps or technical drawings of objects – available, e.g., in the Auto

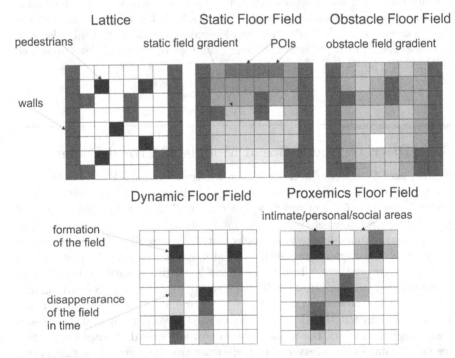

FIGURE 3.7
Examples of basic grids and floor fields: Lattice with moving pedestrians, static floor fields with POIs, obstacle floor field, dynamic floor field (using an analogy to the chemotaxis process), and proxemic floor field.

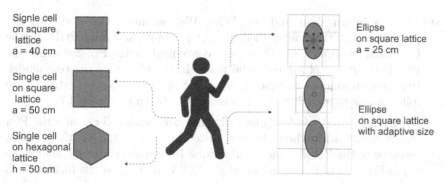

FIGURE 3.8
Popular 2D representations of pedestrians. On the left, two square representations and a hexagonal representation. On the right, elliptical representations of Social Distances Model proposed in [18] and a general case with an adaptive size.

CAD format. In the environment, fragments of space available for pedestrian traffic are indicated, as well as potential targets (POIs) and other components of the environment. In discrete simulations, specialized cell types are defined, such as (MS) movement space, (W) walls, (E) exits, (S) stairs, and (O) obstacles.

Sometimes, in characteristic places, e.g., bottlenecks, a continuous representation of space (and pedestrians) can be used to enable the precise calculation (estimation) of physical parameters, such as pressure, force, and flow, and the particular areas are indicated with assigned pedestrian entrances and exits to connect with the rest of the model [13].

Physical representation of the agent: It is important to ensure that the representation of pedestrians is in line with reality: in particular, the relationship between flow and density should be kept in mind. Of course, individual populations of people differ, there may be children or elderly people in different situations, so the model should be properly calibrated in each situation. Often, based on average densities, people are represented as squares or hexagons, Figure 3.8, for a specific level of the lattice discretization.

It is often justified to reflect more precise geometric relationships in the crowd, then we use an elliptical representation of a pedestrian, which is placed on the grid of a cellular automaton in such a way that the center of the ellipse and the center of the square cell coincide (Figure 3.8). A pedestrian has the ability to turn 45 degrees at a point. We can use the classic model from [18] in which the mesh is 25 *cm*, and the size of the pedestrian's ellipse is compatible with the average size of a person according to the WHO, 22.5 *cm* – semi-major axis and 13.5 *cm* – semi-minor axis.

Definition of intermediate and final POIs: We assume that an agent/ pedestrian has the ability to define intermediate and final POIs. In the CA-based discrete model, the most convenient method of achieving the POI is the use of static potential fields. In the CA-based discrete model, the most convenient method of achieving the POI for a pedestrian is to follow static potential fields. An example is shown in Figure 3.7.

Let us define $dist(c_{ij}, POI)$ as a distance between a cell $c_{i,j}$ and the POI shown in Eq. 3.14, where the normalized number $dist_{max}$ is the greatest distance to the POI from any cell – Eq. 3.15. Finally, the static field value S_{ij} in Eq. 3.16 increases from 0 at the POI to $dist_{max}$ at the furthest cell.

$$dist(c_{ij}, POI) = \min_{(d_x, d_y) \in POI} \sqrt{(d_x - i)^2 - (d_y - j)^2} \qquad (3.14)$$

$$dist_{max} = \max_{\forall(i,j)} dist(c_{ij}, POI) \qquad (3.15)$$

$$S_{ij} = dist_{max} - dist(c_{ij}, POI) \qquad (3.16)$$

Navigation in a dynamic environment: Pedestrians navigate toward the POI using the static potential field as described previously. They can use additional fields, such as the *wall floor field*, to help keep them away from the walls, (Figure 3.15). An important element in crowd models is interaction with other pedestrians: including mechanisms of imitating others, avoiding others in a short distance, or applying the proxemic principles.

An effective mechanism to handle interaction with other pedestrians is pheromone chemo-taxis originated dynamic floor field D_{ij}^t in the time step t [24]. A pedestrian in a cell causes the formation of a dynamic field (Eq. 3.17), while in subsequent time steps, there is a gradual decrease in its intensity (Eq. 3.18). In [19], we proposed the following formulation of a *dynamic floor field* for the Moore neighborhood:

$$D_{ij}^{t+1} = D_{ij}^t - \beta D_{ij}^t + \frac{\beta}{4}(D_{i+1,j}^t + D_{i-1,j}^t + D_{i,j+1}^t + D_{i,j-1}^t +$$
$$+ D_{i+1,j+1}^t + D_{i+1,j-1}^t + D_{i-1,j-1}^t + D_{i-1,j+1}^t) \qquad (3.17)$$

$$D_{ij}^{t+1} = D_{ij}^t - \theta D_{ij}^t \qquad (3.18)$$

where D_{ij} is the value of the dynamic floor field, while $\beta, \theta \in [0, \infty)$] is a constant responsible for the formation and disappearance of the dynamic floor field, as well as a probability element in the pedestrian's movement algorithm, as well as the visibility range of pedestrians. For navigation based on dynamic and static fields, the following formula can be used (proposed by us in [19]):

$$cost(c_{ij}) = S_{ij}^a + (dens(c_{ij}) + \alpha \cdot dist(c_{ij}, POI)) \cdot W \cdot I$$
$$dens(c_{ij}) = e^{\delta \cdot D_{ij}} \qquad (3.19)$$

where the term S^a_{ij} depicts the value of the static potential field with index a of a potential field leading to a POI, $a \geq 1$ is the total number of POIs, $\alpha \in [0, \infty)$ is a weight parameter, $dens(c_{ij})$ is a density in the Moore neighborhood of cell $c_{i,j}$, D_{ij} collects the value of the dynamic field, and $\delta \in [0, \infty)$ is a weight parameter. Next, $dist(c_{ij}, POI)$ is the distance between the cell with the coordinates i and j to the closest POI, W denotes the wall avoiding factor regarding the nearest wall $W = 1.0 + \sigma_W$ with growing values in the wall neighborhood, $\sigma_W \in (0, 1]$, and I is the inertia parameter, where agents prefer to maintain the movement direction as long as possible $I \in (0, 1)$.

When making decisions about the movement for a specific pedestrian/agent, a strategic layer can be distinguished, which determines the choice of a global POI – it represents the pedestrian's abilities. On the other hand, the traffic algorithm at the tactical-operational level is described by decisions about the directions of movement. A simple example taking into account only static and dynamic potential field is shown in Figure 3.9.

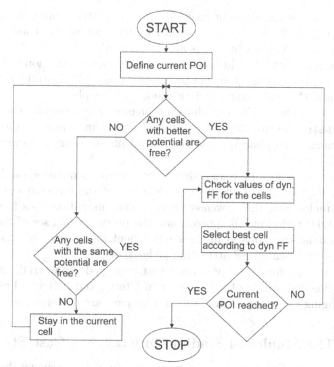

FIGURE 3.9
General view on tactical and operational phase in the movement algorithm using static and dynamic floor fields (dynamic floor field is denoted as dyn FF).

From the point of view of the strategy definition, the process of determining the parameters of the model is important. When modeling a normal situation, pedestrians usually prefer the shorter path, i.e., mutual overtaking is not the dominant pattern, then values of δ are close to 0 (then $dens(f_{ij})$ is close to 1). When values of δ are higher, the situation moves toward competitive evacuation. In this case, due to high densities, blockages often begin to appear.

The addition of further potential fields or groups of pedestrians, as well as detailed decisions at the operational level, results in a significant expansion of the algorithm [19].

3.5   Selected Applications of Crowd Dynamics Models

3.5.1   Lecture Rooms – Case Study

One of the classic examples of crowd dynamics is large room evacuation. On the AGH University in Krakow campus, we have repeatedly conducted such an experiment in various buildings and lecture halls.

The largest room in which we have carried out evacuation experiments many times with various groups of people is the AGH U2 learning center with a lecture hall that can accommodate almost 600 people.

Figure 3.10 shows the two different phases of evacuation, the first one covers pedestrians who have not yet started evacuating (includes the so-called pre-movement time phase), while the second phase covers the evacuation of people.

The next step is to prepare a simulation environment based on AutoCAD drawings. Figure 3.11 shows various elements of the environment, such as walls, obstacles, and the movement space. The simulation uses the level-of-details (LOD) technique to approximate the particular phases of the simulation. Pedestrians are placed in the environment follow selected POIs, which are sources of potential for attracting pedestrians.

Based on the simulation, various statistics on pedestrian traffic are generated. On-line statistics on the frequency of filtering out individual cells of the grid belonging to the set of available traffic space are presented below.

3.5.2   The Municipal Stadium in Krakow – Case Study

From the point of view of the reality/model/simulation scheme (Section 1.1 in Chapter 1), experiments in real conditions are very important. In our work, we use existing databases on pedestrian dynamics, but we also often conduct experiments ourselves, which provide us with valuable data.

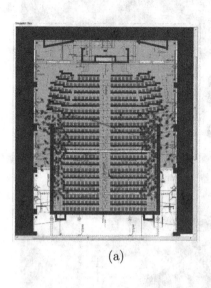

(a)

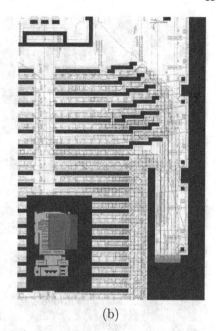

(b)

FIGURE 3.10
Evacuation scenario from the U2 learning center of AGH University of Science and Technology. On the left, experiments with students; on the right, view of agent-based simulation. (a) Evacuated agents are allocated in the simulation environment. (b) Trajectories of evacuated agents.

For the Municipal Stadium in Krakow, research on the analysis of various evacuation scenarios was carried out in cooperation with experts from the association of fire engineers and technicians. In this monograph, I present only examples of data. One can consider several crowd flow scenarios: normal flow, non-competitive evacuation, and competitive evacuation. Figure 3.12 shows the view of the stands during the experiment and then the pedestrian flow in the simulation corresponding to this scenario of non-competitive evacuation.

Another important issue is to determine when the evacuees will leave the facility. The results below describe the flow statistics for 95% of evacuees. Taking into account a non-competitive evacuation scenario for the Municipal Stadium in Cracow, we obtained an evacuation time of 653 s for a group of 11808 pedestrians, when the fastest person evacuated in 3 s and the slowest in 653 s. The desired speed was 1.36 m/s, and the average actual speed was 0.316 m/s.

In Figure 3.13, the statistics from east stands of Municipal Stadium Cracow are presented. On the left – speed distribution and traversed distance, and on the right – distribution of average speed.

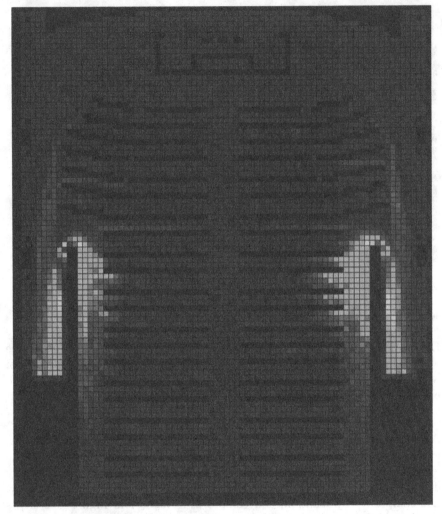

FIGURE 3.11
Statistics of frequency in particular cells during evacuation are visualized.

Such an approach allows calibration to be performed on the basis of general, averaged data for a given type of object and then to verification and validation to be carried out taking into account the scenarios and the specificity of a given object. The end result is a computer simulation that enables for analysis according to given scenarios.

3.5.3   Allianz Arena Munich – Case Study

During a European framework project – Socionical, together with teams from the Technical University of Munich, the University of Passau, ETH Zurich,

(a)

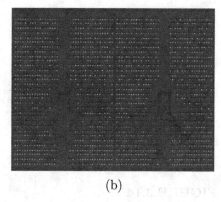

(b)

FIGURE 3.12
Non-competitive evacuation scenario of leaving the stands of the Municipal Stadium in Krakow. (a) Collecting empirical data – two neighboring sectors in the stadium with evacuated fans are visible. Competitive behaviors are not observed. (b) Simulation applied for sectors – the warmer the color, the longer evacuation time from a particular seat

Johannes Kepler University Linz, Vrije Universiteit Amsterdam, and DFKI (German Research Centre for Artificial Intelligence) with the support of Allianz Arena München Stadion GmbH and KVR Kreisverwaltungsreferat Stadt München (KVR) – we modeled the flow of people at the Allianz Arena stadium – in particular, the situation of leaving the stadium. It was a very interesting challenge because in the online regime, it was necessary to simulate the simultaneous flow and behavior of 70000 people. The entire area of the stadium and the surrounding area have been divided into several zones with each having its own specificity. Finally, in the project, we decided to build one

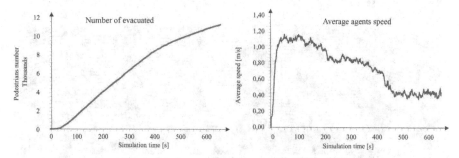

FIGURE 3.13
Distribution of average speed and evacuated persons in time. Statistics for a non-competitive evacuation scenario of leaving the east stands of the Municipal Stadium Krakow.

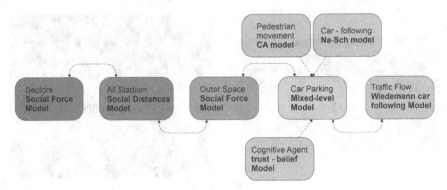

FIGURE 3.14
Simulation server – scheme for modeling of the Allianz Arena Munich stadium.

simulation server for the stadium and the entire area around it, which included various methods of crowd modeling (Figure 3.14). In this chapter, the simulation results for the entire stadium are presented, including the stands for the Social Distances method, in order to get a picture of the whole stadium.

For the *All stadium area*, we have used a modified Social Distances Model [20] based on Cellular Automata and agents (as described in previous sections) to simulate the entire stadium, while for some areas we used different methods. An exemplary view of the evacuation scenario for the Allianz Arena stadium is shown in Figure 3.15

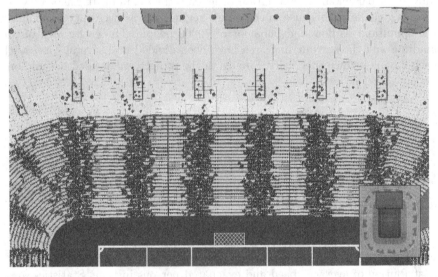

FIGURE 3.15
Simulation of pedestrian flow in the Allianz Arena Munich stadium, using a modified Social Distances Model.

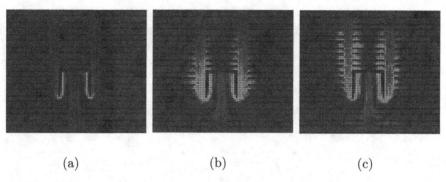

(a)   (b)   (c)

FIGURE 3.16
Sample statistics for flow in the stands of Allianz Arena Munich are presented: frequency matrix of flowing agents for the three following scenarios: (a) normal situation – low fluctuations, (b) non-competitive evacuation – moderate fluctuations, and (c) competitive evacuation – high fluctuations.

Depending on the simulated situation, namely a normal situation, competitive evacuation, or non-competitive evacuation, we obtained various statistics on the flow of people. In particular, one can notice differences in frequency matrices (Figure 3.16c). In normal situations, the flow is stabilized and fluctuations are low. During non-competitive evacuation, an increase in the occurrence of fluctuations can be seen – their level is moderate, and during competitive evacuation, high fluctuations are clearly noticeable.

An important statistic is the comparison of average speeds over time and the number of evacuees over time. The charts below show the evacuation statistics for a normal situation (Figure 3.17), non-competitive evacuation (Figure 3.18), and competitive evacuation (Figure 3.19).

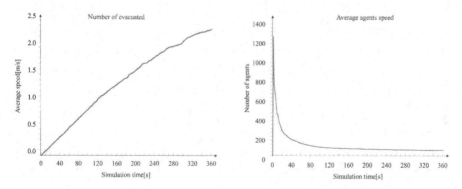

FIGURE 3.17
Simulation of pedestrian flow in Allianz Arena Munich stadium, using modified Social Distances Model – normal situation.

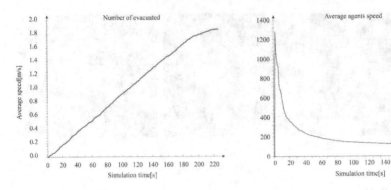

FIGURE 3.18
Simulation of pedestrian flow in Allianz Arena Munich stadium, using modified Social Distances Model – non-competive situation.

Regarding quantitative outputs of the simulation we take into account population of 1305 pedestrians allocated in a sector, the desired speed for normal conditions was $\mu = 1.1\ [m/s]\ \sigma^2 = 0.26$, while for non-competitive and competitive evacuation $\mu = 1.34\ [m/s]\ \sigma^2 = 0.26$. The evacuation time was the shortest for competitive evacuation 218 s (average speed was 0.311 [m/s], and average density and average flow for two available exits were 3.00/2.74 $[P/m^2]$ and 3.13/2.85 $[P/s]$, respectively), the next was result of non-competitive evacuation 226 s (average speed was 0.170 [m/s], and average density and average flow for two available two exits – 3.61/3.08 $[P/m^2]$ and 3.03/2.74 $[P/s]$, respectively), and the longest evacuation time was for normal conditions 361 s (average speed was 0.101 [m/s], and average density and average flow for two available two exits – 1.86/1.55 $[P/m^2]$ and 1.89/1.71 $[P/s]$, respectively).

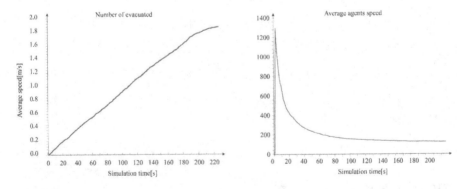

FIGURE 3.19
Simulation of pedestrian flow in Allianz Arena Munich stadium, using modified Social Distances Model – competitive situation.

For the non-competitive and competitive evacuation, we can observe higher density, especially around the emergency exits in comparison to the normal conditions scenario. Similarly, one can notice a difference in average speed and average flow, which result in shorter evacuation times. In competitive and non-competitive evacuation, we can observe a more active process of the decision-making and way-finding processes (Figure 3.16).

Taking into account non-competitive evacuation scenario for the Allianz Arena, we have received for 580000 pedestrians evacuation time 1117 s, when the fastest person evacuated in 2 s and the slowest in 1117 s. The desired speed was 1.36 m/s, and the average actual speed was 0.316 m/s. These results were achieved for the 95% fastest evacuees.

3.6 Verification and Validation

An important element is the simulation verification and model validation. An example of a standard that supports *Validation and Verification* is the ISO/TR13387-8 Technical Report. It includes the following stages: component testing (taking into account software engineering methods), functional validation (checking of model capabilities), qualitative verification (predicted behaviors versus expectations), and quantitative verification (comparison of quantitative data from the model versus reality). We have validated and verified all models, for instance an exemplary fundamental diagram, i.e., the flow-to-density relation, is presented in Figure 3.20. Compressibility coefficient *eps* is 0, which means we do not assume compressibility of pedestrians.

3.7 Discussion

Modeling a complex system with a collective characteristic, such as crowd dynamics and behavior modeling, is a difficult and demanding task. When it comes to creating simulations for engineering applications, the key is to define specific scenarios for which to conduct the simulation and ensure that all layers of the agent's decision-making level ensure compliance in the physical flow of agents (according to the rules of physics), e.g., the relationship between flow and density is satisfied. A very interesting scheme that we used in the modeling project of the Allianz Arena stadium is the definition of several classes of situations: normal situation, non-competitive evacuation, and competitive evacuation. This allowed the most important features to be extracted from the cognitive agent level to the transition function operating on the physical level responsible for the movement of agents. Similar effects were achieved in

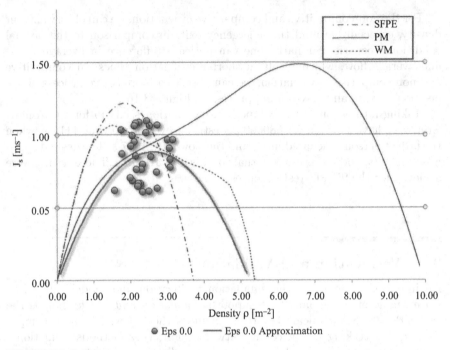

FIGURE 3.20
Fundamental diagram of pedestrian flow in a modified Social Distances Model used for the simulation of crowds for stadium scenarios. Compressibility factor Eps = 0.0. Reference diagrams: SFPE – Society of Fire Protection Engineers, PM – Predtetschenski and Milinski, WM – Weidemann.

the form of modeling of dynamic POI determination for agents, i.e., a strategic decision-making function that could be dynamically defined in individual pedestrian traffic scenarios.

Bibliography

[1] Alfano, V.: Is democracy possible without a restriction of the suffrage? Studia Humana **3**(3), 3–10 (2014). https://doi.org/10.2478/sh-2014-0009

[2] Bon, G.L.: The Crowd [Tr. From Psychologie des Foules]. Alcan (1896)

[3] Forsyth, D.R.: Group Dynamics. Cengage, Boston (2019)

[4] Teknomo, K., Gerilla, G.: Mesoscopic multi-agent pedestrian simulation. In: P.O. Inweldi (ed.) Transportation Research Trends, pp. 323–336. Nova Science Publisher, New York (2008)

[5] Kormanová, A.: A review on macroscopic pedestrian flow modelling. Acta Inform. **2**, 39–50 (2013). https://doi.org/10.18267/j.aip.22

[6] Helbing, D.: A fluid dynamic model for the movement of pedestrians. Complex Systems **6**, 43–52 (1998)

[7] Daamen, W., Hoogendoorn, S., Bovy, P.: First-order pedestrian traffic flow theory. PHL **1**, 1–14 (2005). https://doi.org/10.3141/1934-05

[8] Hughes, R.: The flow of large crowds of pedestrians. Math. Comput. Simul. **53**, 367–370 (2000). https://doi.org/10.1016/S0378-4754(00)00228-7

[9] Fruin, J.J.: Designing for pedestrians: A level-of-service concept. Highway Research Record (1971)

[10] Bratman, M.: Intention, Plans, and Practical Reason. Harvard University Press, Cambridge, MA (1987). URL http://books.google.de/books?id=I0nuAAAAMAAJ

[11] Newell, A.: The knowledge level. Artif. Intell. **18**(1), 87–127 (1982). https://doi.org/10.1016/0004-3702(82)90012-1. https://www.sciencedirect.com/science/article/pii/0004370282900121

[12] Helbing, D., Farkas, I., Molnar, P., Vicsek, T.: Simulation of Pedestrian Crowds in Normal and Evacuation Situations, vol. 21, pp. 21–58. Springer, Berlin, Heidelberg (2002)

[13] Tytko, K., Mamica, M., Pękala, A., Wąs, J.: Simulating pedestrians' motion in different scenarios with modified social force model. In: R. Wyrzykowski, E. Deelman, J. Dongarra, K. Karczewski (eds.) Parallel Processing and Applied Mathematics. PPAM 2019. Lecture Notes in Computer Science, vol 12044, pp. 467–477. Springer, Cham (2020). https://doi.org/10.1007/978-3-030-43222-5_41

[14] Lakoba, T., Kaup, D., Finkelstein, N.: Modifications of the helbing-molnár-farkas-vicsek social force model for pedestrian evolution. Simulation **81**, 339–352 (2005). https://doi.org/10.1177/0037549705052772

[15] Moussaïd, M., Helbing, D., Garnier, S., Johansson, A., Combe, M., Theraulaz, G.: Experimental study of the behavioural mechanisms underlying self-organization in human crowds. Proc. R. Soc. B: Biol. Sci **276**, 2755–2762 (2009). https://doi.org/10.1098/rspb.2009.0405

[16] Moussaïd, M., Helbing, D., Theraulaz, G.: How simple rules determine pedestrian behavior and crowd disasters. Proc. Natl. Acad. Sci. U.S.A. **108**, 6884–6888 (2011). https://doi.org/10.1073/pnas.1016507108

[17] El Yacoubi, S., El Jai, A.: Cellular automata modelling and spreadability. Math. Comput. Model. **36**(9), 1059–1074 (2002). https://doi.org/10.1016/S0895-7177(02)00259-5.   https://www.sciencedirect.com/science/article/pii/S0895717702002595

[18] Wąs, J., Gudowski, B., Matuszyk, P.J.: Social distances model of pedestrian dynamics. In: S. El Yacoubi, B. Chopard, S. Bandini (eds.) Cellular Automata, pp. 492–501. Springer, Berlin, Heidelberg (2006)

[19] Wąs, J., Lubaś, R.: Towards realistic and effective agent-based models of crowd dynamics. Neurocomputing **146**, 199–209 (2014). https://doi.org/10.1016/j.neucom.2014.04.057.   https://www.sciencedirect.com/science/article/pii/S0925231214007838

[20] Wąs, J., Lubaś, R.: Adapting social distances model for mass evacuation simulation. J. Cell. Autom. **8**(5/6), 395–405 (2013)

[21] Lubaś, R., Wąs, J., Porzycki, J.: Cellular automata as the basis of effective and realistic agent-based models of crowd behavior. J. Supercomput. **72**, 2170–2196 (2016). https://doi.org/10.1007/s11227-016-1718-7

[22] Bazior, G., Pałka, D., Wąs, J.: Using cellular automata to model high density pedestrian dynamics. In: V.V. Krzhizhanovskaya, G. Závodszky, M.H. Lees, J.J. Dongarra, P.M.A. Sloot, S. Brissos, J. Teixeira (eds.) Computational Science – ICCS 2020, pp. 486–498. Springer International Publishing, Cham (2020)

[23] Bandini, S., Federici, M.L., Vizzari, G.: Situated cellular agents approach to crowd modeling and simulation. Cybern. Syst. **38**(7), 729–753 (2007). https://doi.org/10.1080/01969720701534141

[24] Nishinari, K., Kirchner, A., Namazi, A., Schadschneider, A.: Extended floor field CA model for evacuation dynamics. IEICE Trans. **87-D**, 726–732 (2008). http://dblp.uni-trier.de/db/journals/ieicet/ieicet87d.html

4

Car Traffic Modeling

4.1 Basics of Modeling and Simulation of Car Traffic

A long time has passed since the creation of the first car, which was a three-wheeled and two-seated car "Motorwagen" patented by Karl Benz on 29 January 1886. The vehicle equipped with a gasoline engine had a four-stroke engine with an output of 0.55 kW, which corresponded to a power of 0.75 horsepower [1]. The maximum speed of the car was about 16 km/h. The fuel, which was ligroin or gasoline, was available at that time only in pharmacies (ligroin was originally used as a stain remover). In 1888, the wife of car inventor, Bertha Benz, made her first major journey from Mannheim to Pforzheim and back for a total of 180 km – the first car journey of such length [1]. Since then, the rapid development of the automotive industry has continued. According to current statistics (kept by Hedges & Company), at the end of the first quarter of 2022, there were 1.45 billion vehicles registered in the world, of which 1.1 billion were passenger cars [2]. Considering that there were around 7.9 billion people in the world in 2022, statistically speaking, there is one car for 7.18 people.

The structure of vehicle propulsion types has changed over time; more and more newly registered vehicles have hybrid or electric propulsion or are powered by alternative energy sources (e.g., hydrogen). For example, in the European Union in 2021, newly registered cars had the following drive systems: 40% petrol, 19.6% diesel, 19.6% hybrid electric (HEV), 9.1% battery electric (BEV), and 8.9% plug-in-hybrid (PHEV) [3]. So, one can observe a process of breaking away from traditional drives toward electric, hybrid, and alternative drives. At the same time, the share of newly registered BEV + PHEV + HEV vehicles increased from 11.7% in 2019, through 22.4% in 2020, to 37.6% in 2021. Simultaneously, Advanced Driver Assistance Systems (ADAS) supporting the driver are increasingly popular and the achievement of successive degrees of vehicle autonomy can be observed. These threads have been discussed in our papers [4–6].

4.1.1 Road Traffic Measurements and Basic Concepts

Currently, three main methods of obtaining traffic data can be distinguished:

DOI: 10.1201/b23388-4

- measurements with the use of induction loops – in particular double loops that enable the measurement of sectional speed

- measurements with the use of video image recognition techniques

- measurements using position sensors (GPS) based on smartphone data collected from road users

There are three basic types of road traffic, depending on the traffic intensity: free flow, synchronized flow, and wide moving jam. The last two types of flow are termed congested traffic.

Some basic terms behind traffic modeling can be described as follows:

Flow is the number of cars passing a specific place per unit of time. The maximum possible flow on a given road is called road capacity.

Distance-headway is the distance between the given point of the moving car and the exact same point of the car in front. $d_n = v_n(t_n - t_{n-1}) - l_{n-1}$ where v – speed of a car n, t – time and l – length of a car.

Time-headway is the time interval between the arrival of two consecutive cars to a certain fixed point. $t_h(n) = t_n - t_{n-1} - \frac{l_{n-1}}{v_{n-1}}$ where v – speed of a car n, t – time and l – length of a car.

Density is the ratio of flow to average speed. $\rho = \frac{J}{v}$ where J is flow and v is average speed. The relation between the density ρ, $flow$, and velocity v derives from hydrodynamics and is called a fundamental diagram [7].

4.1.2   Existing Approaches in Car Traffic Modeling

The most important classification of traffic models is the vehicle representation. In microscopic models, vehicles are represented as individual particles with individual properties and parameters assigned to them, while in macroscopic models we treat motion similar to the dynamics of liquids or gases.

One of the most famous traffic models is the Nagel-Schreckenberg model, constructed using a one-dimensional cellular automaton. In this model, the road is divided into equal sections with a length of 7.5 m and time step equal $dt = 1$ s. Each cell can contain exactly one car or be empty. The car moves at the speed given in the number of cells per time step. The top speed in the Na-Sch model is 33.3 m/s, which translates into a value of approximately 120 km/h (namely 119, 88 m/s).

The Na-Sch model algorithm consists of 4 steps (Eq. 4.1):

1. Velocity – it is increased by the value of one, if the current speed is not maximal: $v_{t+1} \rightarrow min(v_t + 1, 0)$

2. Slowing down – if the distance between two consecutive cars is smaller than the velocity of the car located at the front, the car

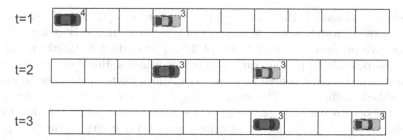

FIGURE 4.1
Sample configuration of cars in consecutive time steps in the Nagel-Schreckenberg model.

in the rear brakes to a speed equal to the number of free cells between these vehicles: $v_{t+1} \to min(v_t - 1, 0)$

3. Randomization – if the speed of a car is equal or greater than 1, its speed is reduced by one unit with the probability of 1: $v_{t+1} \to max(v_t - 1, 0)$

4. Motion of a car – each car moves forward with a speed equal to the number of cells at a speed equal to the number of passed/visited cells during one time step: $x_{t+1} \to max(x_t + 1, 0)$

The presented traffic rules are very simple; however, they realistically present the nature of traffic on a road with one lane (Figure 4.1). From the point of view of the realism of the simulation, the third step of randomization is important as it introduces an element of randomness related to different types, drivers' reactions, or unexpected situations on the road.

One can point out different popular models of car traffic.

The Velocity-Dependent-Randomization (VDR) model. In the classic Na-Sch model, it is not possible to reproduce the slow-to-start phenomenon in which drivers start with a delay after stopping, e.g., in front of traffic lights. This results from the delayed reaction of drivers and is a very common phenomenon in road traffic. A modification of the Na-Sch model was proposed to handle this situation [8]. In this model, the third step of the Na-Sch model was modified by introducing a parameter p, which determines the probability depending on the current vehicle speed. In this model, the head of the vehicle is operated as a normal object in the Na-Sch model, and the rest of the vehicle is moved by exactly the same amount as the head.

$$p(v) = \begin{cases} p_0 & \text{for} \quad v = 0 \\ p & \text{for} \quad v > 0 \end{cases}$$

where $p_0 > p$

Leading head model. Hartman in [9] proposed reducing the size of a single cell to more accurately reflect the nature of the traffic. In the Hartman model, the division into cells with a size of 2.5 m was adopted, thanks to which it was possible to present various types of vehicles. However, in this case, most vehicles must consist of many cells, which leads to the need to apply modified traffic rules. The work of Hartman proposed that a motorcycle should occupy one cell, a passenger car – 2 cells, and a larger vehicle – more cells, respectively. An important consequence is the change in the real speed of the car in relation to the speed in the model. The speed of a car moving, e.g., 3 cells per second, was 81 km/h in the original Na-Sch model, and only 18 km/h in the model with 2.5 m cells. Hartman also described another element often found in modern cities: the roundabout. He treated the space around as a model example of a straight road that has only common elements with access roads.

The Intelligent Driver Model (IDM). Daimin Tang, Xiang Li, and Yijuan Jiang [10] presented a microscopic model of traffic. The model is capable of handling different road situations, including acceleration, driving in normal traffic, following and approaching other cars, the appliance of traffic lights, and usage of collision avoidance mechanisms. In the IDM, each vehicle determines its speed depending on the difference between its speed and the speed of the preceding car $\Delta v_n = v_{n+1} - v_n$ and the distance $d_n = x_{n+1} - x_n - l$, where velocity can be calculated as follows (Eq. 4.1):

$$\dot{v}_n = a \left[1 - \left(\frac{v_n}{v_0} \right)^{\delta} - \left(\frac{d_n^*}{d_n} \right) \right] \tag{4.1}$$

In this equation, a is maximum acceleration, v_0 is desired speed, d is minimum desired headway, and δ is acceleration exponent. The desired spatial gap depends on the speed of the car and its increment: $d_n^*(v_n, \Delta v_n) = d_0 + T v_n - \frac{v_n \Delta v_n}{2\sqrt{ab}}$, where d_0 is typical traffic jam interval, T_n is safe interval, and b is comfortable delay. The expression $\frac{v_n \Delta v_n}{2\sqrt{ab}}$ introduces the intelligent braking strategy, namely models dynamic, gentle braking of the vehicle, while approaching the vehicle in front.

4.2   Proposed Traffic Model

The classic Na-Sch model, created by Kai Nagel and Michael Schreckenberg in 1992 [11], is dedicated to simulating road traffic on highways or expressways. In the model, traffic within one lane is considered.

The advantage of the original Na-Sch model is its simplicity, but it has numerous limitations due to its application characteristics: 7.5 m cell (vehicle

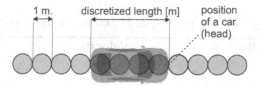

FIGURE 4.2
Representation of space and vehicles in the proposed model.

length), no lane change mechanism, no intersections and roundabouts, several possible speed values, as well as constant and unrealistic acceleration value. Over the years, many developments of the model were created, where different, individual mechanisms were added: [8] [12–14] and so on.

Modern cars have different lengths: for example, medium lengths[1] urban cars are of the average length 3.7 *m*, compact cars about 4.25 *m*, family automobiles about 4.55 *m*, a full-size SUV 4.95 *m*, while the dimensions of trucks range from 6 to 18.75 *m* (road trains)[2]. This means, in practice, that more accurate discretization is welcome in models.

4.2.1 Basic Assumptions of the Proposed Model

Realistic values of acceleration and deceleration of vehicles in traffic are compared in [15], [16]. Namely the average acceleration of a standard passenger car is most often equal 1.5 $m/s \pm 0.5$, while in the case of a truck 1.2 $m/s \pm 0.4$. Our team has also proposed several models and carried out a number of implementations in the last dozen or so years starting from [17], through agent representation of vehicles [18], ending with very detailed models for the passage of emergency vehicles [19].

Representation of space. To refine the representation of road sections, we assumed a cell size equal to 1 *m*, where each vehicle may consist of several cells (Figure 4.2).

A road network is a collection of cells out of which every single cell has information about its neighbors, i.e., the cell in front (next), the cell behind (previous), and the cells on the left or right, if any. This makes it possible to create roads with many lanes and to connect the ends of two separate roads so that they can pass between them. A single cell can be either *occupied* or *empty*. The vehicle currently occupies the number of consecutive cells equal to its length expressed in meters. All occupied cells change their status in this way to occupied.

---

[1] According to https://carroar.com/car-length/
[2] According to OECD transport regulations in most European countries https://www.itf-oecd.org/sites/default/files/docs/dimensions-2019.pdf

TABLE 4.1
Velocity Values for the Interval Equal to 500 ms in the Adopted Model.

Number of cells	Velocity $\dfrac{m}{s}$	Velocity $\dfrac{km}{h}$
10	20	72
9	18	64.8
8	16	57.6
7	14	50.4
6	12	43.2
5	10	36
4	8	28.8
3	6	21.6
2	4	14.4
1	2	7.2

Representation of time and speed. We assume the time step $dt = 0.5$ s The introduction of the division of the road into 1 m cells allows various speeds and lower accelerations to be obtained than in the unrealistic one in the original Na-Sch model (7.5 m/s^2). The model does not have a maximum speed limit, as this value is determined for each road separately. In Table 4.1, values of vehicle speed in the model are presented. These are only selected values as there is no upper speed limit.

Environmental analysis. The behavior of each vehicle depends on the current traffic situation. For this purpose, a behavior variable has been introduced, which can take one of the values presented in Eq. 4.2:

$$behavior = \begin{cases} -2 & \text{when hard braking is required} \\ -1 & \text{when gentle braking is required} \\ 0 & \text{when the current speed should be maintained} \\ 1 & \text{when acceleration is required} \end{cases} \quad (4.2)$$

The behavior of a given vehicle is determined by many circumstances on the road. In the simplest case, it depends on the distance d from the vehicle in front and the speed of both vehicles v_n, v_{n+1}. Based on the values of d and v_{n+1}, the d_{real} distance is calculated as $d_{real}(d; v) = d + b(v)$, where $b(v)$ is the hard braking distance from v to zero. The vehicle behind determines its behavior on the basis of its own speed v and the d_{real} distance – Figure 4.3.

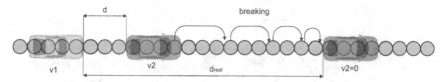

FIGURE 4.3
Distance d as the distance between two driving vehicles c_1 and c_2 and distance d_{real} as the sum of d and the sudden braking distance of the vehicle c_2.

4.2.2 Proposed Modification of the Rules of the Na-Sch Model

In order to better reflect traffic in urban conditions, the rules of the Nagel model have been modified, (Eq. 4.3). All the rules are gathered together.

1. Randomization – braking probability parameter p (for instance $p = 0.15$).

$$behavior_{t+1} = \begin{cases} max(behavior_{t+1} - 2, -2) & \text{if the car is not being} \\ & \text{brought into traffic} \\ behavior_{t+1} & \text{if the car is being} \\ & \text{brought into traffic} \end{cases}$$

$$(4.3)$$

2. Acceleration or Braking Speed is defined using the following formula (Eq. 4.4)

$$v_{t+1} = \begin{cases} max(v_t - dec, 0) & \text{if } behavior < 0 \\ v_t & \text{if } behavior = 0 \\ min(v_t + acc, v_{max}) & \text{if } behavior > 0 \end{cases} \quad (4.4)$$

3. Driving ($x_{t+1} \rightarrow x_t + v_{floor}$). The step adding the traffic randomness element does not change the value of v but only modifies the *behavior*. Contrary to the Na-Sch model, it is made at the very beginning. In this step, the behavior value is reduced by 2 with a given probability, which in the case of accelerating cars results in gentle braking, in the case of cars that want to maintain the current speed results in sudden braking; however, it does not change the behavior of vehicles that are forced to brake aggressively (such behavior has the lowest possible value). Acceleration and braking are performed in the same time step. As a result, the speed v is increased or decreased by a certain amount depending on the behavior and type of vehicle. The behavior is described in previous parts of Section 4.2.

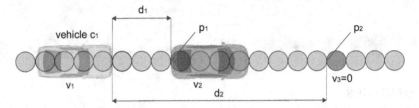

FIGURE 4.4
Graphical representation of the obstacle search by the vehicle c_1 – two obstacles were found: the vehicle driving in front p_1 and the blocked cell of a special type (p_2).

4.2.3 Movement Algorithm

We assume that there are two types of obstacles on the road: the first is static objects (stop lines – traffic lights, objects placed on the road such as bollards or other stationary obstacles that are not road users) and moving objects, i.e., other road users (Figure 4.4. The following symbols are applied in this description: p_1 – position of dynamic obstacle (vehicle in front), p_2 – position of static obstacle (red traffic light), d_1 – distance to p_1, and d_y – distance to p_2. Additionally, the sight of vehicle n: $s(n) = db_{normal}(v_n) + v_n$, where db_{normal} is normal breaking distance from v_n to 0 and v_n is speed of vehicle n. A dynamic obstacle is formulated as $d_1 = db_{em}(v_1)$, while a static obstacle d_2.

The vehicle's sight range is equal to its gentle braking distance [18], and the search for obstacles ends when the last cell in the sight line is reached or when obstacles of various types have already been found, i.e., a vehicle or a special cell type. Special types of cells are places that are blocked whether or not a vehicle is occupying them. They can be treated as obstacles but can also be ignored by some vehicles. The following special type cells can be distinguished:

traffic light cells – points controlled by traffic lights (their state depends on the signaling cycle). Cycle time and switch time are taken into account (Figure 4.5). Sample systems with traffic lights are presented in Figure 4.6,

priority points – places where the right-of-way should be taken into account (their visibility is determined individually for an oncoming vehicle),

extreme points – marked places where one should change the lane in order to follow a given route.

There is often a situation where roads intersect or a minor road joins a major road. Thus, we have two kinds of checkpoints: entering points, Figure 4.7, where vehicles enter a main road, and crossing points where vehicles only cross the road line (Figure 4.8). d_1 is distance which c_1 has to cover to pass a checkpoint, and d_2 is distance which c_2 has to cover to reach a checkpoint.

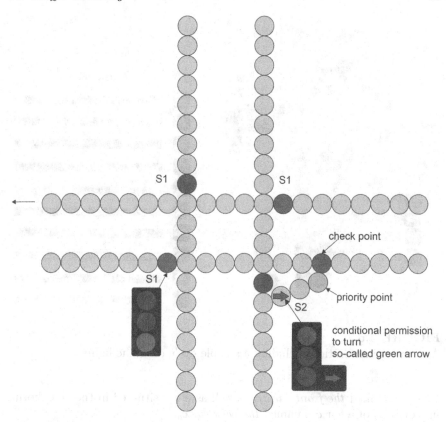

FIGURE 4.5
View on intersection representation using traffic lights, including a conditional green arrow, check point, and priority point.

Safety criteria can be defined as follows:

- entering point: Will c_1 cover distance d_1 before c_2 covers d_2 and then they won't collide?

- crossing point: Will c_1 cover distance d_1 before c_2 covers d_2?

An important mechanism in the model is the lane change mechanism. The scheme is presented in Figure 4.9 One can point out two main motivations to change lane, when this action is:

- profitable – the goal is to overtake a slower vehicle

- necessary – to reach a certain point on the road map

In the model, there is a safety criterion, Eq. 4.5, taking into account cars on a neighboring line, namely a car situated in the neighboring line in front of

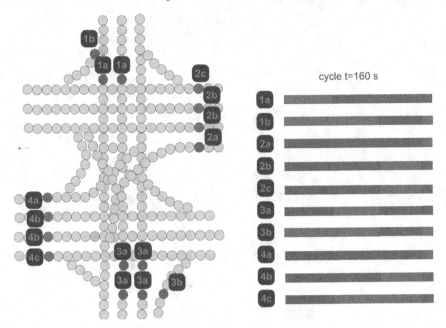

FIGURE 4.6
A complex intersection including a sample cycle of traffic lights.

a car c – named *the front car* c_f, as well as a car situated in the neighboring line in front of a car c – named *the back car* c_b:

$$\begin{cases} b(v_b) + d_1 - len > b(v) \\ b(v) + d_2 > b(v_f) \end{cases} \tag{4.5}$$

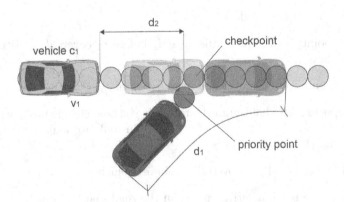

FIGURE 4.7
An entering mechanism for road connections.

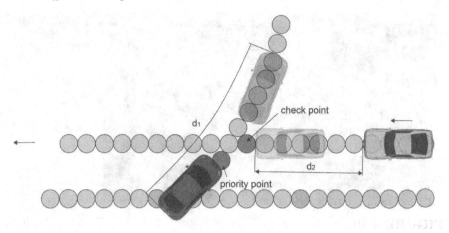

FIGURE 4.8
A crossing point mechanism for road connections.

where $b(v_b), b(v),$ and $b(v_f)$ are emergency braking distances of vehicles $c_b, c,$ and c_f, respectively.

Figure 4.10 shows the configuration of the simulation environment. A grid of the simulation environment has been marked on the map, taking into account all traffic directions as well as traffic lights.

Initially, the number of vehicles grows to the point where it reaches a certain value (approx. 500 *vehicles*), around which it oscillates until the end of the simulation. The time until a steady state is reached is called the warm-up time. In the test, the simulation warmed up for approx. 1200 iterations (approx. 10 *min*); therefore, the *Warm-Up Period* parameter was set to 10 *min*. Only after this time, all simulation measurements are saved – i.e., after starting the simulation.

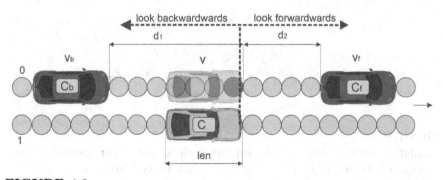

FIGURE 4.9
Change line mechanism.

FIGURE 4.10
Simulation setup – road. An example of Opolska Street in Krakow.

The simulation environment is presented in Figure 4.10. During the simulation, the number of vehicles is recorded as well as the time when new vehicle positions are calculated. The data are stored in the *calculation time* table where the index corresponds to the iteration number. The graph presenting the number of vehicles on the roads during the simulation is shown in the figure.

We take into account the following part of Krakow for tests (Figure 4.11) located in Azory/Prądnik Biały Districts with Opolska Street as a communication axis.

An example of a simulation image with visible vehicles is shown in Figure 4.12. This is Opolska/Wyki Streets' cross-section. Various types of vehicles with visible lights at an intersection are presented for each route.

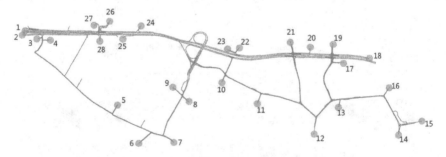

FIGURE 4.11
Simulation setup – road configurations with allocated car generators. An example of the city of Kraków (Azory/Prądnik Biały Districts).

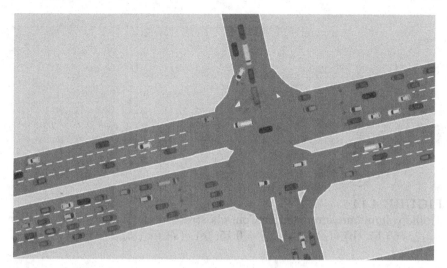

FIGURE 4.12
Sample simulation screen for Opolska Street (intersection with Wyki Street).
The current status of lights with passing vehicles is displayed.

4.2.4   Measurement of Traffic Volumes

Road traffic was examined in three arbitrarily selected places, with measurement places shown in Figure 4.13.

We have taken into account the following parameters; specific flow J, density ρ and v, as well as their dependencies, formulated in the form of fundamental diagrams.

The first set of figures with the fundamental diagrams for checkpoint a located in Conrada Street is presented in Figure 4.14.

The next set of figures with the fundamental diagrams presented for checkpoint b located in Opolska Street is presented in Figure 4.15.

FIGURE 4.13
Location of measuring points where the vehicle flow was measured – city of Kraków (Azory/Prądnik Biały Districts).

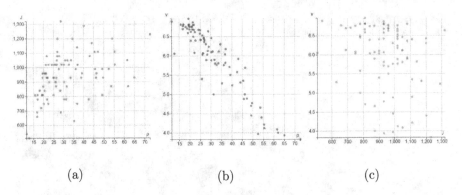

FIGURE 4.14
Traffic volume measurement for Conrada street at checkpoint a. (a) $J(\rho)$ for $p_{break} = 0.15$. (b) $v(\rho)$ for $p_{break} = 0.15$. (c) $v(J)$ for $p_{break} = 0.15$.

The next set of figures with the fundamental diagrams presented for checkpoint c located in Krowoderskich Zuchów Street is presented in Figure 4.16.

At checkpoint a – located in Conrada Street, the maximum flow was just over 1300 *vehicles/h* on a single lane, while the minimum flow was 400 *vehicles/h*. The maximum density ρ did not exceed 70 *vehicles/km* in such congestion, traffic is described as unstable, encountered in the event of a sequence of short traffic jams. The average speed of vehicles at this point ranged between 4 and 7 *m/dt* which (between 28 and 50 *km/h*). At checkpoint b – located in Opolska Street, the maximum flow was approx. 1100 *vehicles/h*,

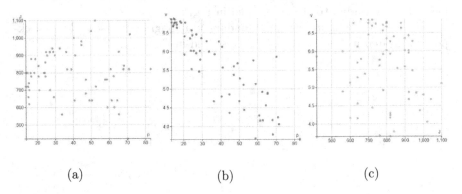

FIGURE 4.15
Traffic volume measurement for Opolska street at checkpoint b. (a) $J(\rho)$ for $p_{break} = 0.15$. (b) $v(\rho)$ for $p_{break} = 0.15$. (c) $v(J)$ for $p_{break} = 0.15$.

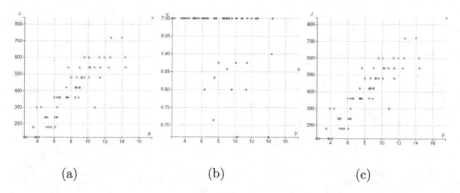

(a)   (b)   (c)

FIGURE 4.16
Traffic volume measurement for Krowoderskich Zuchów Street at checkpoint c.
(a) $J(\rho)$ for $p_{break} = 0.15$. (b) $v(\rho)$ for $p_{break} = 0.15$. (c) $v(J)$ for $p_{break} = 0.15$.

and the minimum flow was 500 *vehicles/h* (on a single lane). The minimum density was approx. 10 *vehicles/km*, while the maximum density was 80 *vehicle/km* (at a speed of approx. 3.5 m/dt, i.e., 25 km/h). The average speed ranged between 3.5 and 7 m/dt (i.e., between 25 and 50 km/h). At checkpoint c located at Krowoderskich Zuchów Street, the maximum flow was 800 *vehicles/h* and the minimum flow was only 100 *vehicles/hour*. The maximum traffic density was 18 vehicles/km (which corresponds to approaching an unstable flow). The average speed remained at the level of the maximum speed $v_{max} = 7$ m/dt or slightly below this value (the minimum speed was approx. 6.65 m/dt or approx. 48 km/h).

4.2.5 Calculation Time with Increased Traffic Volume

In order to measure the calculation time in the simulation, in each iteration the data were written in the table including $[n; t_n]$, where n is number of vehicles, and t_n is time of calculating new vehicle positions. Vehicle generator settings have been modified to obtain as many vehicles as possible in the simulation area. The purpose of the test was to measure the simulation efficiency in the event of extreme traffic congestion. On the basis of the obtained times, the calculation of the dependence $t(n)$ was made. This is shown in Figure 4.17. The computation time increases with the increase in the number of vehicles, but the time increase is milder in the case of high traffic congestion. This fact is related to the dependence of the length of the vehicle's field of view on the speed with which it is driving. In the event of heavy traffic, vehicles move at a low speed, which reduces the time needed to calculate the position of a single vehicle due to the analysis of the smaller field of view of this vehicle.

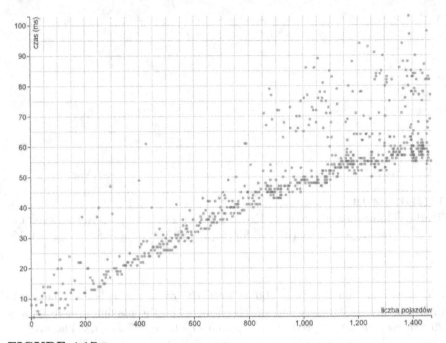

FIGURE 4.17
Graph showing the dependence of the calculation time on the number of vehicles

4.3   Verification and Validation

We take into account the following different aspects in the process of validation and calibration. First, in order to verify the correctness of the model, a test generating graphs of the dependence J, ρ, and v was performed. In the road editor, a closed road (the end of the road is connected to its beginning) with a length of approx. 5 km was created. At one point in the road, a vehicle generator was set up that generated 900 vehicles per hour. Cars that appeared on the road began to circle around the loop and gradually congested the traffic. At the other end of the loop, a checkpoint was created. The simulation was carried out until the maximum vehicle compaction on the road, which occurred approx. 1.5 h after the start of the simulation. The parameters adopted in the test were $p_{break} = 0.25$ (probability of random braking) and $v_{max} = 7$ (maximum speed).

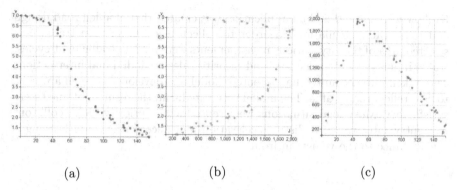

(a)   (b)   (c)

FIGURE 4.18
Fundamental diagrams from experiments. $J(\rho)$, $V(\rho)$, and $v(J)$, where $J_{max} \approx 1800\frac{vehicles}{hour}$ $\rho_{max} \approx 170\frac{vehicles}{hour}$. (a) Relationship speed vs. density. (b) Relationship speed vs. specific flow. (c) Relationship between specific flow and density.

We have analyzed fundamental diagrams taking into account c_f flow, c_v velocity, and c_d density. We have used the following formulas (Eq. 4.6):

$$\begin{aligned}
\text{Flow} \qquad & J_n = c_f \frac{60}{dt_m n_{lanes}} & [veh/h/lane] \\
\text{Velocity} \qquad & v_n = \frac{c_v}{c_f} & [m/dt] \\
\text{Density} \qquad & \rho_n = \frac{c_d}{dt_m \cdot 60 \cdot ips \cdot n_{lanes}} \frac{1000}{d_m} & [veh/km/lane]
\end{aligned} \qquad (4.6)$$

where dt_m denotes measurement time, d_m denotes measurement distance, n_{lanes} denotes number of lanes, and ips denotes iterations per second.

Fundamental diagrams are presented in the following figures (Figure 4.18):

The maximal recorded flow is achieved for a density of $40-45\ vehicles/km$, and the maximum possible density is $160-170\ vehicles/km$.

The time until a steady state is reached is called the warm-up time. In our tests, the simulation was warmed up for about 1200 iterations.

4.4 Discussion

The aim was to develop a model of road traffic dynamics effective in the simulation of urban areas. After analyzing the existing models, an urban traffic model based on the Nagel-Schreckenberg model was proposed. Modifications introduced in the model adapted it to urban conditions. The next phase of the project was testing the model. For this purpose, a part of the city of

Krakow was selected and an application was created that enabled road design and road traffic simulation. In order to collect accurate data on traffic in a selected area of the city, various measurements were made – traffic light cycles, traffic intensity, route selection, and priority rules for individual intersections were taken into account. The presented model was developed in such a way as to best reflect road traffic. The model was tested, and the results obtained were satisfactory. Most road situations were reproducible: priority yield, collision-free entry into traffic, realistic acceleration and deceleration, and keeping a safe distance to the vehicle in front.

Bibliography

[1] Mercedes-Benz, G.: 1885–1886: The first automobile. https://group.mercedes-benz.com/company/tradition/company-history/1885-1886.html

[2] Bonicci, D.: How many cars are there in the world? https://www.whichcar.com.au/news/how-many-cars-are-there-in-the-world

[3] T.E.A.M. Association: Fuel types of new passenger cars in the EU. https://www.acea.auto/figure/fuel-types-of-new-passenger-cars-in-eu/

[4] Szlachetka, M., Borkowski, D., Wąs, J.: The downselection of measurements used for free space determination in ADAS. J. Comput. Sci. **63**, 101,762 (2022). https://doi.org/10.1016/j.jocs.2022.101762. https://www.sciencedirect.com/science/article/pii/S1877750322001454

[5] Szlachetka, M., Borkowski, D., Was, J.: Stationary environment models for advanced driver assistance systems. In: 2020 Signal Processing: Algorithms, Architectures, Arrangements, and Applications (SPA), pp. 116–121 (2020). https://doi.org/10.23919/SPA50552.2020.9241306

[6] Pikus, M., Wąs, J.: The application of virtual logic models to simulate real environment for testing advanced driving-assistance systems. In: 2019 24th International Conference on Methods and Models in Automation and Robotics (MMAR), pp. 544–547 (2019). https://doi.org/10.1109/MMAR.2019.8864634

[7] Kerner, B.S.: Three-phase traffic theory. In: M. Fukui, Y. Sugiyama, M. Schreckenberg, D.E. Wolf (eds.) Traffic and Granular Flow, pp. 13–50. Springer, Berlin, Heidelberg (2003)

[8] Barlovic, R., Santen, L., Schadschneider, A., Schreckenberg, M.: Metastable states in cellular automata for traffic flow. Eur. Phys. J. 5, 793–800 (1998)

[9] Hartman, D.: Head leading algorithm for urban traffic modeling. 16th European Simulation Symposium, pp. 10–17. SSC Press (2004)

[10] Tang, D., Li, X., Jiang, Y.: Microscopic traffic simulation oriented road network data model. In: 2010 2nd International Conference on Future Computer and Communication, vol. 2, pp. V2-87–V2-91 (2010). https://doi.org/10.1109/ICFCC.2010.5497347

[11] Nagel, K., Schreckenberg, M.: A cellular automaton model for freeway traffic. J. phys., I **2**(12), 2221–2229 (1992). https://doi.org/10.1051/jp1:1992277

[12] Nagel, K., Wolf, D.E., Wagner, P., Simon, P.: Two-lane traffic rules for cellular automata: A systematic approach. Phys. Rev. E **58**, 1425–1437 (1998). https://link.aps.org/doi/10.1103/PhysRevE.58.1425

[13] Helbing, D., Farkas, I., Molnar, P., Vicsek, T.: Simulation of Pedestrian Crowds in Normal and Evacuation Situations, vol. 21, pp. 21–58. Springer (2002)

[14] Schadschneider, A., Schreckenberg, M.: Traffic flow models with 'slow-to-start' rules. Ann. Phys. **509**, 425–444 (1997)

[15] Bonsall, P., Liu, R., Young, W.: Modelling safety-related driving behaviour - impact of parameter values. Transp Res Part A Policy Pract **39**, 425–444 (2005). https://doi.org/10.1016/j.tra.2005.02.002

[16] Treiber, M., Kesting, A.: Traffic Flow Dynamics, pp. 239–255. AGH Publishing House, Krakow (2013)

[17] Wąs, J., Bieliński, R., Gajewski, B., Orzechowski, P.: Issues of city traffic modeling based on cellular automata. Automatyka **13**, 1207–1217 (2009)

[18] Chmielewska, M., Kotlarz, M., Wąs, J.: Computer simulation of traffic flow based on cellular automata and multi-agent system. In: R. Wyrzykowski, E. Deelman, J. Dongarra, K. Karczewski, J. Kitowski, K. Wiatr (eds.) Parallel Processing and Applied Mathematics, pp. 517–527. Springer International Publishing, Cham (2016)

[19] Małecki, K., Kamiński, M., Wąs, J.: A multi-cell cellular automata model of traffic flow with emergency vehicles: Effect of a corridor of life and drivers' behaviour. J. Comput. Sci. **61**, 101, 628 (2022). https://doi.org/10.1016/j.jocs.2022.101628. https://www.sciencedirect.com/science/article/pii/S1877750322000515

5

Modeling Dynamics of Downhill Skiers

5.1 Basics of Modeling and Simulation of Skiing

Skiing is an activity known to people for many thousands of years. The Encyclopedia Britannica reports that the oldest skis found in the world come from 8000–7000 BC. Skiing was practiced as an effective means of transport in cold and temperate climates.

Over the last few decades, many forms of skiing have evolved, such as cross-country skiing, biathlon, acrobatic skiing, ski jumping, and finally downhill skiing. It should be emphasized that in the last dozen or so years, the development of carving skis has resulted in the fact that downhill skiing has become a mass sport. This has had many significant effects. First of all, the development of the ski base has not kept pace with the increase in the number of skiers, which means that many ski resorts are highly crowded. As a consequence, we observe many accidents, many of which are very dangerous, leading to death or permanent disability. For instance, in Austria, 369 fatalities of skiers were reported between 2008 and 2018 [1]. As the statistics show, the most serious accidents occur in 80–85% of cases on blue (easy) and red (moderate) routes, while only 5–8% on black (hard) and the remaining cases on undefined routes [1].

The number of skiers in the world has increased from 115 million to 135 million in the last 8 years. For instance, each of world's three most popular ski resorts, Campiglio Dolomiti di Brenta, Ski Arlberg, and La Plagne, is visited by nearly 2.5 million skiers annually [2]. Currently, about 36% of people in Austria are active skiers; however, the total number of skiers is 2.96 million. Countries with the highest number of skiers in Europe are: Germany (14.6 million), France (8.5 million), Italy (7.2 million), UK (6.3 million), and Poland (4.9 million)[1].

As a result, in recent years, many activities related to increasing the level of safety on the ski slopes have been undertaken. The interest in computer simulation as a method of analyzing skiing safety has also increased because computer simulations provide important information from the point of view of security planning.

---

[1]https://www.statista.com/statistics/801008/europe-number-of-people-skiing-by-country/

DOI: 10.1201/b23388-5

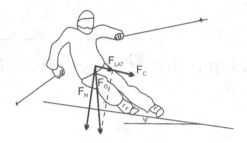

FIGURE 5.1
The sense and direction of the centripetal force depending on the turn stage.

A number of physical forces act on a skier on a ski slope. The most important ones are presented in Figure 5.1. A skier is represented as an object with a mass m, a position r, a direction of movement e, and a speed v.

There are two main types of turn in modern downhill skiing: skidded and curved. Schemes of both are presented in Figure 5.2 When a skier performs a

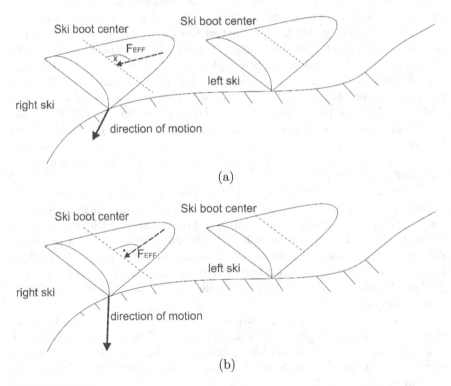

FIGURE 5.2
Two main types of turns in skiing: skidded and curved. (a) Mechanism of skidded turns. (b) Mechanism of curved turns.

skidded turn, the angle χ between the effective force F_{EFF} of a skier is greater than a right angle (90 degrees), due to this mechanism, the skis slide to the side [3].

The movement of skiers has a specificity related to the sliding movement of skis on the snow surface – the key role is played by the component resulting from the force of gravity. After reaching the appropriate height (using a ski lift or climbing the hill) and initiating the movement, the skier, generally speaking, converts the potential energy into the kinetic energy of the movement. It is a different nature of traffic from a physical point of view than in classic pedestrian dynamics. The basic mechanism here is the dynamic mapping of the route depending on the set goals, terrain obstacles, routes and types of snow, and finally the location of other skiers.

5.2   How to Model Skiers' Dynamics

Two types of forces related to skiing can be distinguished: one of them is social forces, which describe the skier's path toward way-points (intermediate POIs) and the second group are physical forces (related to gravity, centrifugal force, friction, etc.) [3].

In [4], we presented a model of downhill skiing based on a modified and adapted SFM (Social Force Model). In this model, the desired direction of movement can be calculated as $e_{social} = \frac{F_{social}}{\|F_{social}\|}$, where F_{social} represents the net force of all social forces.

One can say, that skier α will turn in e_{social} direction if $e_{social} \times e_{\alpha} \leqslant cos(\delta)$ and we assume that δ is an angle with a constant value.

If the angle between the current direction of movement e and desired direction e_{social} is greater than δ, then the skier will perform a turn – such a situation is presented in Figure 5.3. In the presented case, this is a right turn. The mechanism is based on the solution proposed in [3].

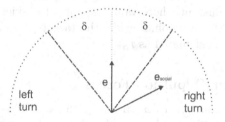

FIGURE 5.3
The current direction of movement e and desired direction e_{social} is greater than δ; thus, the skier will perform a right turn.

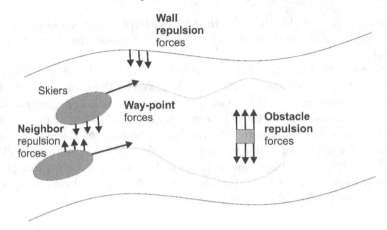

FIGURE 5.4
Social Forces of particular skiers.

Skiers' Social Forces can be divided into four different groups with the idea shown in Figure 5.4.

A convenient scheme that enables the construction of an effective simulation of a skier's dynamics is to create a model analogous to that of the Social Force method, taking into account various forces acting on the skier. This approach has been used in our article [4].

5.2.1   Way-Point Forces

In order to create an effective and realistic simulation, it is best to assume that the skier sets new way-points while riding. There are forces associated with way-points that guide the skier toward which the skier is going. At the end of the route, the final way-point is marked at which the skier stops. A convenient method is to use a constant value way-points and consequently to direct them toward the set goals and to properly direct their trajectory of movement. We can write this force as $F_{waypoint} = A_0 = \frac{r_{\alpha w}}{\|r_{\alpha w}\|}$. In this equation, A_0 is a constant whose value indicates the skier's determination to reach the consecutive way-points, while the target position between skier r_α and way-point r_w is calculated as $r_{\alpha w} = r_w - r_\alpha$.

5.2.2   Neighbor Repulsion Forces

One of the most important rules on a slope for a skier is to maintain a safe distance from other skiers and to avoid collisions. In the model, the force responsible for maintaining safe distances and avoiding collisions is the neighbor repulsion force. The solution to the repulsive forces between neighbors, which we adopted in [4] is based on forces in the Social Distances Model presented

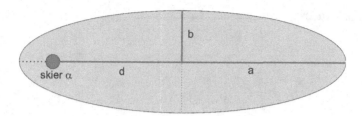

FIGURE 5.5
Social ellipse of skier α.

in [5] by J. Wąs, B. Gudowski, and P. J. Matuszyk. Skiers travel at much faster speeds (recreational skiers $15-40\ km/h$), than pedestrians during normal traffic ($3-7\ km/h$), so the consequences of a potential collisions can be very serious during downhill skiing.

For this reason, it is reasonable that the safety zone around the skier should be an ellipse, and its size should be determined by *the current speed* of the skier. The ellipse around a skier α is presented in Figure 5.5. The ellipse is characterized by a – semi-major axis of the ellipse, b – semi-minor axis of the ellipse, d – distance from the center of the ellipse to the skier α position, $b = r_0$, where r_0 is a radius of the social area for a skier α moving with $v = 0$, $a = b + s_v v$, where s_v is a factor of scale for v, $d = \frac{v}{v_{max}}\sqrt{a^2 - b^2}$, where v_{max} is the fastest possible speed of a skier.

Skiers' ellipse sizes depend on the current skiers' speed. In Figure 5.6, one can notice different sizes of ellipses. An important issue is the geometric relationships and their relation to speed, namely when the skier is moving at speed v, then the distance from the skier to the focal point of the ellipse equals $\sqrt{a^2 - b^2}$. The figure above shows the shapes of ellipses for $\|v\| = 0, \|v\| = 10\ m/s, \|v\| = 20\ m/s$, and $\|v\| = 50\ m/s$:

The key issue in the adopted model is the interaction between skiers. Considering the situation where we have two skiers α and β, the repulsion force will act from the β skier only when the α skier is inside the β skier's ellipse (the β skier is in the α skier's field of view). In a situation where the α skier is at the boundary of the ellipse (social area) of the β skier, then the direction of the forces is a vector normal to the ellipse at the point of contact and a vector directed opposite to the vector $r_{ac=r_c-r_\alpha}$ (where r_c is the position of the center of the β skier's social ellipse). Basically, when we have skier β and skier α in his/her social ellipse, then the direction of the repulsive force can be defined as follows: $e_{neighbor} = \frac{-r_{ac}}{\|r_{ac}\|}$. In a situation where the skier's β speed is greater than 0, the skier's position does not coincide with the center of the skier's social ellipse, and the distance between the skier position and the center of his/her social ellipse can be calculated according to the above mentioned equation $d = \frac{v}{v_{max}}\sqrt{a^2 - b^2}$. So, we can assume that the neighbor repulsion force allows collisions to be avoided between skiers and is defined

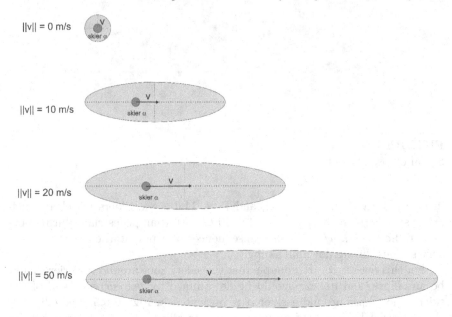

FIGURE 5.6
Social ellipse of skier α for different values of current speed.

similarly to the Social Distances Model [5]. One of the key terms in the skiers modeling case is the distance $r_{normalized}$ defined in the interval $[0,1]$. Thus, the force $f_{neighbor}$ can be described as $f_{neighbor} = F_i(r_{normalized})e_{neighbor}$, where F_i is a scheme of social sources between agents from [5]. The forces are presented in Figure 5.7. In the power version, the following model of forces is applied: $F_s(r) = \frac{F_{max}(r-1)}{\frac{\alpha-0.5}{\alpha}(2r)^n-1}$.

The case with multiple skiers is worth considering, i.e., if a given skier α falls within the social ellipses of several other skiers, then the net force is determined as the sum of the forces from individual skiers.

5.2.3   Obstacle Repulsion Forces

The force responsible for avoiding a collision and maintaining a safe distance from static obstacles, like electricity poles, cable-way supports, trees, and restaurants on the slopes, is the *Obstacle repulsion force*.

It is defined in the same way as the neighbor repulsion force and however is determined for static objects. In practice, this means that these objects are marked on the simulation map, and during the simulation, repulsion force is calculated for them, assuming that their speed is equal to zero.

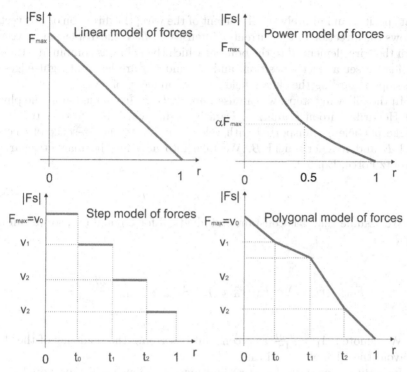

FIGURE 5.7
Repulsion forces between skiers according to [5].

5.2.4 Slope Edge Repulsion Forces

These are the forces that keep the skier on the ski slope, keeping the distance to the border of the route and prevent the skier from falling outside the slope. There are several possibilities to draw a physical analogy to such repulsion forces. We used the idea of the adapted Biot-Savart law with an analogy to magnetic field B from our work [4] in order to simulate pushing the skier away from the edge of the ski run. In the original, the equation makes it possible to determine the value and direction of the induction vector of the magnetic field $d\vec{B}$ generated by a conductor element of length $d\vec{l}$ carrying current I. In our case, the edges of the route are described by two wires that induce a magnetic field and keep the skier on the route. This is calculated using Eq. 5.1 according to vector notation of the Biot-Savart law.

$$\vec{B}(\vec{r_\alpha}) = \frac{\mu_0}{4\pi} \int_{C_L + C_R} \frac{I d\vec{l} \times \vec{r'}}{|\vec{r'}|^3} \tag{5.1}$$

In this equation, μ_0 is the magnetic constant, interpreted as permeability of free space $\mu_0 = 4\pi 10^{-7} Teslam/A$, I is the steady current, $d\vec{l}$ is the vector that specifies an infinitely small element of the wire, the direction of this vector follows the direction of the current of intensity I, $d\vec{r'}$ is the displacement vector from the wire element $d\vec{l}$ to the point at which the field was computed – thanks to this we set a skier's position, and C_L and C_R are left and right edges of the slope regarding the skier's field of view (analogy of wires).

In the following steps, we can use *Lorentz Force* (so named after the physicist Hendrik Antoon Lorentz of Danish origin) which is a force acting on a charge particle q transported with velocity v due to the presence of electric field E and magnetic field B. We take into account the magnetic part of Lorentz Force, Eq. 5.2:

$$\vec{F}_M(\vec{r_\alpha}, \vec{v}_\alpha) = q\vec{v}_\alpha \times \vec{B}(\vec{r_\alpha}) \tag{5.2}$$

We assume that I is constant and identical for C_L and C_R, so we can use Eq. 5.3:

$$\vec{F}_{edges}(\vec{r_\alpha}, \vec{v}_\alpha) = \vec{F}_M(\vec{r_\alpha}, \vec{v}_\alpha) = A_1\vec{v}_\alpha \times \int\limits_{C_L+C_R} \frac{d\vec{l} \times \vec{r'}}{|\vec{r'}|^3} \tag{5.3}$$

We denoted $A_1 = \frac{\mu_0 q I}{4\pi}$ as a constant describing the tendency of the skier to avoid the edge of the ski run.

In addition, we introduce two limiting conditions for the proposed social forces. The first limits the field of view of skiers to a proper distance, while the second limits the angle of view. In the first case, $d_{visibility}$ describes visibility conditions on the ski slope (Eq. 5.4), which can be limited by fog or snowfall; additionally, a skier can ignore an object located at a certain distance.

$$u(\vec{r}, d_{visiblity}) = \begin{cases} 1, & \text{if } \|\vec{r}\| \leq d_{visiblity} \\ 0, & \text{otherwise} \end{cases} \tag{5.4}$$

In the second case, a viewing angle can be reduced according to Eq. 5.4. The second limiting function is the reduction of the angle of view φ. This takes the form presented in Eq. 5.5

$$w(\vec{r_1}, \vec{r_2}) = \begin{cases} 1, & \text{if } (\vec{r_1}/\|\vec{r_1}\|) \cdot (\vec{r_2}/\|\vec{r_2}\|) \geq \cos(\varphi) \\ 0, & \text{otherwise} \end{cases} \tag{5.5}$$

We can reformulate the repulsion forces taking into account the field of view Eq. 5.4 and Eq. 5.5, and finally we can formulate Eq. 5.6.

$$\begin{aligned} \vec{F}_{neighbor}(\vec{r}_\alpha, \vec{r}_\beta, \vec{v}_\alpha, \vec{v}_\beta) &= u(\vec{r}_{\alpha\beta}, d_{visibility})w(\vec{v}_\alpha, -\vec{r}_{\alpha\beta})\vec{f}_{neighbor} \\ \vec{F}_{obstacle}(\vec{r}_\alpha, \vec{r}_o, \vec{v}_\alpha) &= u(\vec{r}_{\alpha o}, d_{visibility})w(\vec{v}_\alpha, -\vec{r}_{\alpha o})\vec{f}_{obstacle} \end{aligned} \tag{5.6}$$

In this context, we can formulate the final equation (Eq. 5.7):

$$\vec{F}_{social} = \vec{F}_{waypoint}(\vec{r_\alpha}) + \sum_\beta \vec{F}_{neighbor}(\vec{r_\alpha}, \vec{r_\beta}, \vec{v_\alpha}, \vec{v_\beta}) +$$
$$\sum_o \vec{F}_{obstacle}(\vec{r_\alpha}, \vec{r_o}, \vec{v_\alpha}) + \vec{F}_{edges}(\vec{r_\alpha}, \vec{v_\alpha}) \tag{5.7}$$

In [4], we introduced three additional mechanisms of a skier's social behavior. The first one is speed reduction when the safe speed limit for the skier is exceeded. This is done by initiating a brake (skid) turn. The second behavior is to perform a braking maneuver when reaching the end of the slope. The key parameters here are the safe limit speed and safe braking distance, which are parameterized depending on the level of the skier's skill. The third behavior is accelerating force, which is initialized when the speed drops below the minimum speed v_min. Then, the skier uses ski poles (or skating steps).

5.2.5 Characteristics of Physical Forces in Skiing

A skier is a physical object characterized by mass, velocity, position, and direction of motion. One can point out the main forces during skiing with the basic scheme presented in Figure 5.8

We used the following forces in [4] in order to simulate skiers. The description of the forces is placed in Table 5.1.

One can point out centrifugal force and lateral force, which together constitute the total transverse force. The diagram of forces depending on the turning phase is shown in Figure 5.9.

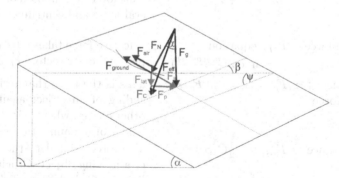

FIGURE 5.8
Forces acting on a skier.

TABLE 5.1
The Set of Forces Acting on Skiers in a Modified Social Forces Approach.

Type of force	Physical formula	Description
Downhill force	$\vec{F}_n = mg\cos(\alpha)\vec{n}$ $$\vec{F}_g = mg \begin{bmatrix} 0 \\ 0 \\ -1 \end{bmatrix}$$	Defined in an inclined plane with an α slope. Two components – perpendicular to the pressure force $\vec{F}_n$ and parallel to the downhill force of descent $\vec{F}_s$ – make up the force of gravity force $\vec{F}_g$. Here $\vec{n}$ is a normal vector to surface in point $\vec{r}$
Parallel downhill force	$\vec{F}_p = mg\sin(\alpha)\sin(\beta)\vec{e}$	Downhill force's component $\vec{F}_s$ parallel to the ski run. Angle β is situated between the direction of motion and a line parallel to the slope line $\beta \subseteq [0, 180]°$
Lateral force	$\vec{F}_{lat} = \vec{F}_s - \vec{F}_p$ $F_{lat} = mg\sin(\alpha)\cos(\beta)$	The force is perpendicular to slope direction defined in downhill force $\vec{F}_s$. One can calculate the value of vector F_{lat}
Centrifugal force	$\vec{F}_c = \frac{m}{R}\|\vec{v}\|^2\vec{e}_N$	It is the apparent outward force acting on a skier during a turn, where R is a radius of turning and $\vec{e}_N$ is the unit vector normal to the skier's trajectory
Total transverse force	$\vec{F}_{tl} = \vec{F}_c + \vec{F}_{lat}$	This force is composed of the lateral force and centrifugal force
Effective force	F_{eff} equation [a] $\phi = \arccos(\frac{mg\cos(\alpha)}{F_{eff}})$	Effective force takes into account perpendicular vectors $\vec{F}_{tl}$ and $\vec{F}_N$
Kinematic friction force	$\vec{F}_{ground} = -\mu\|\vec{F}_{eff}\|\vec{e}$	This is the force that resists the sliding of an object against another object, where μ is the coefficient of dynamic friction
Air resistance force	$\vec{F}_{air} = -\frac{1}{2}C_dS_d\|\vec{v}\|^2\vec{e}$	The force related to the surface of a moving object. Crucial coefficients: C_d is drag coefficient, S_d projected frontal area of the object, and ρ represents air density
Net force	$\vec{F}_{net} = \vec{F}_p + \vec{F}_{air} + \vec{F}_{ground}$	The force gathering all forces

[a] – Effective force $F_{eff} = \sqrt{(\frac{m}{R}\|\vec{v}\|^2 \pm mg\sin(\alpha)\cos(\beta))^2 + (mg\cos(\alpha))^2}$

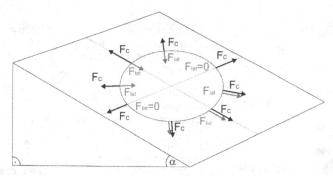

FIGURE 5.9
Characteristic of centrifugal and lateral forces depending on the turning phase.

5.3   Sample Simulations of Downhill Skiing

We have taken into account one of the longest ski routes in Poland, namely route no. 1 in Jaworzyna Krynicka, with a length of about 2600 m and mean angle of inclination of 18%. This route is mainly served by a gondola with a maximum capacity of 1600 people per hour [4]. According to the actual scheme, the gondola takes skiers to the top of the Jaworzyna Krynicka mountain in 6-person gondolas and then the skiers start descending at a low speed of 0–5 m/s. We assume that the speed on the whole slope is in the range from 0 to 30 m/s [6]. For some parameters, we used a normal Gaussian distribution marked as gaussian(μ, σ).

5.3.1   Parameters of Skiers and Physical Constants

Parameters and constants applied in simulation can be divided into three main groups: Ski lift (gondola) parameters, skiers parameters, and physical constants. The main parameters are shown in Figure 5.10.

Regarding the Social Forces, we applied a step model (Figure 5.7) with the following parameters: $F_{max} = 1200, v_1 = 1080, v_2 = 120, t_0 = 0.33$, and $t_1 = 0.66$.

We take into account the following characteristics of skiers' motion: the first is *mean velocities* in amateur skiing, where we can assume a range from 0 to 90 km/h, the second is *the most visited places* – the warmer the color, the more willingly the place is visited, and the third are *the average distances between skiers* where we use a scale between 0 and 12 m.

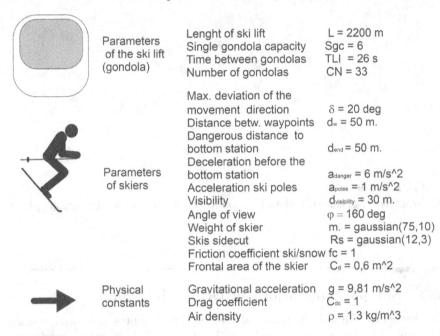

Parameters of the ski lift (gondola)	Lenght of ski lift	L = 2200 m
	Single gondola capacity	Sgc = 6
	Time between gondolas	TLI = 26 s
	Number of gondolas	CN = 33
Parameters of skiers	Max. deviation of the movement direction	δ = 20 deg
	Distance betw. waypoints	d_w = 50 m.
	Dangerous distance to bottom station	d_{end} = 50 m.
	Deceleration before the bottom station	a_{danger} = 6 m/s^2
	Acceleration ski poles	a_{poles} = 1 m/s^2
	Visibility	$d_{visibility}$ = 30 m.
	Angle of view	φ = 160 deg
	Weight of skier	m. = gaussian(75,10)
	Skis sidecut	Rs = gaussian(12,3)
	Friction coefficient ski/snow	fc = 1
	Frontal area of the skier	C_d = 0,6 m^2
Physical constants	Gravitational acceleration	g = 9,81 m/s^2
	Drag coefficient	C_{dc} = 1
	Air density	ρ = 1.3 kg/m^3

FIGURE 5.10
The main parameters applied during simulation.

5.3.2 Characteristics of Ski Lifts

The key element of modern downhill skiing is a system of ski lifts connected with a network of ski slopes and a system of artificial snowmaking. Modern ski lifts include various types of equipment: from local carpet lifts and T-bar lifts to technically advanced chair lifts and gondolas. An important parameter is the *capacity* of the ski lifts, as this translates into the density of skiers (and snowboarders) on the slope and is a factor that affects safety. The capacity is the parameter that represents the maximum number of skiers/snowboarders who can be transported in a time unit. Other crucial parameters are lift length L_{length}, carrier size CS, number of carriers CN, and arrival of carriers in time $loadI$.

Thus, the distance from one chair to the next chair can be described as $cD = \frac{2*L_{length}}{CN}[m]$. The speed of a lift can be calculated as $L_{speed} = \frac{cD}{loadI}[m/s]$. Total travel time from the bottom to upper station of the ski lift can be calculated as $t_T = \frac{L_{length}}{L_{speed}}[s]$. We can also point out the number of people transported in one hour by a chair-lift $N_h = \frac{3600}{t_T*2}$.

In order to calculate capacity, we can use the following formula: $L_{capacity} = N_h * cAm * cS = \frac{3600*cS}{loadI}[people/h]$, where cAm is the carrier amount.

5.3.3 Sample Results of Simulations

Our simulation lasted 2 *h* each run. We marked pink obstacles. During the first run, we generated 100 skiers. The results are visible in Figures 5.11 and 5.12.

During the first simulation, the average speed of skiers was approximately 9.8 *m/s*.

In the second example, we changed the value of the friction coefficient up to 0.03 and 0.04 in turn. This corresponds to the type of skiing conditions, i.e., snow characteristics: "slow snow" vs. "fast snow". In this case, the average speed was 11.52 *m/s*.

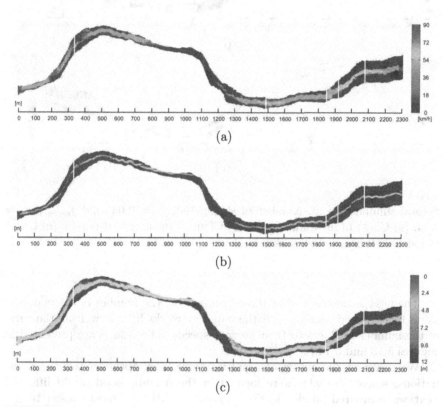

FIGURE 5.11
The first run of simulation. The following parameters are applied: total number of skiers: 100, $f_c = 0.05$, and $f_{c-turning} = 0.06$. (a) Statistics of medium speeds. (b) Statistics of most visited places. (c) Statistics of mean distances between skiers.

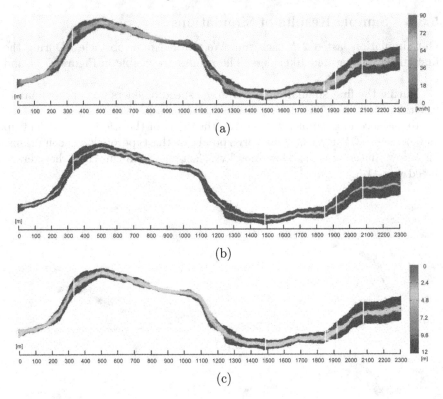

(a)

(b)

(c)

FIGURE 5.12
Second simulation run. Number of skiers: 100, $f_c = 0.03$, and $f_{c-turning} = 0.04$. (a) Chart of medium speeds. (b) Chart of most visited points. (c) Chart of mean distances between skiers.

The next issue was to test the dependence of the number of skiers on the slope (on selected sections) on the capacity of ski lifts as well as the ratio of the number of skiers to their average speeds. The results are presented in Figures 5.13 and 5.14.

We analyzed the acting of repulsion force from obstacles in special situations, where obstacles were located in the neighborhood of ski lift, and next we compared single skier's trajectories with the most-chosen trajectories in the course of many simulations. The comparison is shown in Figure 5.15.

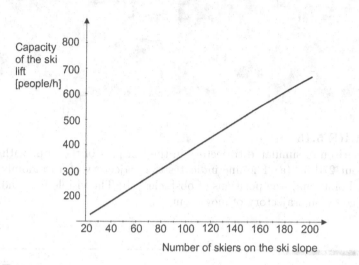

FIGURE 5.13
Relationship between the number of skiers and lift capacity.

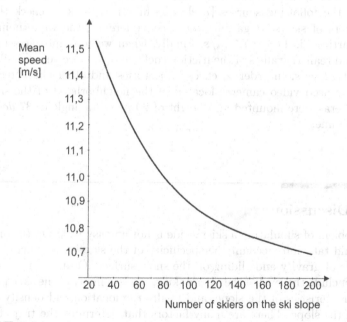

FIGURE 5.14
Relationship between the number of skiers and average speed.

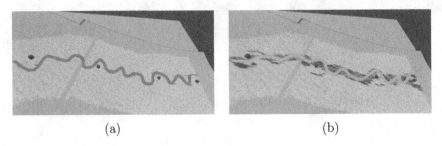

(a)   (b)

FIGURE 5.15
Comparison of simulated trajectory in the last part of the slope with a length
of about 270 m. (a) The line indicates the trajectory of a randomly selected
skier. Points map the positions of obstacles. (b) The visible lines indicate the
most common trajectory of movement.

5.4   Verification and Validation

As a case study for our work, we used the *Jaworzyna Krynicka* ski complex
located in the health resort of Krynica Zdrój (southern Poland). In order to
validate and verify the characteristics of the skiers' mobility, we took into
account the following sources [7–9]. The first issue was to check the basic
parameters of skiers. Regarding the speed reference, the value pointed out
by the articles is 11.4 ± 1.5 m/s. Finally, when we took into account social
forces and realistic values of the friction coefficient, we received a similar value
of about 12 m/s. In order to check trajectories and other characteristics of
skiers, we used video cameras located in the neighborhood of the ski route.
The cameras were mounted at a height of 20 m at an angle of 37 *degrees* to
the slope line.

5.5   Discussion

The problem of simulating a skier's ride is not an easy task. On the one hand,
we should take into account the specificity of the skier's movement based on
the force of gravity and sliding on the snow surface. On the other hand, key
factors include the level of the skier's skills, the specificity of the ski equipment,
the characteristics of the slope, and finally the location and density of other
users of the slope. There are many factors that determine the trajectory of a
ride.

The edge-pushing model proposed in this chapter, based on the Biot-Savart
law and Lorentz Force, takes into account the distance and shape of the entire

edge of the slope, not just the nearest points – it allows for realistic navigation and adaptation to the edge of the route by the skier.

In the model, there is a rule that at low speeds there is a small repulsion force from the edge of the slope, which increases with speed. An important feature of the model is that the skier can run parallel along the edge of the slope. Why? Because the repulsion force depends, in addition, on the angle between the velocity vector and the vector representing the element of the edge of the slope, and if the measure of the angle is 0 or 180 degrees, the repulsion force is equal to 0. This makes it possible to simulate high-density situations and exclude the effect of pushing skiers to the middle of the slope as in the Holleczek-Tröster model.

As a result of the work, a continuous model was developed that adapts the methods of social forces and social distances for downhill skiing.

The limitation of the model is that we have adopted the carving turn as the main one, although while keeping smaller turning radii, it is possible to estimate sliding turns. In addition, extended validation of the model on a larger scale would definitely be useful. It is quite a time-consuming and costly operation, but it would allow for further development of the model.

A very important element is the delineation of social zones around skiers in the shape of ellipses (depending on the current speed of skiers), which makes it possible to explain the distance between skiers traveling at different speeds. The model takes into account the slope end braking mechanism with realistic deceleration parameters for us, which are values of the order 13 m/s.

We took into account the mechanism of pushing off with poles (or moving with a skating step). The results showed a good resemblance of the model to reality, despite the limitations of the model.

Bibliography

[1] Posch, M., Schranz, A., Lener, M., Burtscher, M., Ruedl, G.: Incidences of fatalities on Austrian ski slopes: A 10-year Analysis. Analysis. Int. J. Environ. Res. Public Health 2916. https://doi.org/10.3390/ijerph17082916

[2] Vanat, L.: 2021 international report on snow and mountain tourism. https://www.vanat.ch/RM-world-report-2021.pdf (2021). 13th edition

[3] Holleczek, T., Tröster, G.: Particle-based model for skiing traffic. Phys. Rev. E **85**, 056, 101 (2012). https://link.aps.org/doi/10.1103/PhysRevE.85.056101

[4] Korecki, T., Pałka, D., Wąs, J.: Adaptation of social force model for simulation of downhill skiing. J. Comput. Sci. **16**, 29–42 (2016).

https://doi.org/10.1016/j.jocs.2016.02.006.   https://www.sciencedirect.
com/science/article/pii/S1877750316300138

[5] Wąs, J., Gudowski, B., Matuszyk, P.J.: Social distances model of pedestrian dynamics. In: S. El Yacoubi, B. Chopard, S. Bandini (eds.) Cellular Automata, pp. 492–501. Springer, Berlin, Heidelberg (2006)

[6] Lind, D., Sanders, S.: The physics of skiing : skiing at the Triple Point. American Institute of Physics, Woodbury, NY (2004)

[7] Shealy, J., Ettlinger, C., Johnson, R.: How fast do winter sports participants travel on alpine slopes? J. ASTM Int. **2** (2005). https://doi.org/10.1520/JAI12092

[8] Waegli, A., Skaloud, J.: Turning point. trajectory analysis for skiers. Inside GNSS (Spring 2007) (2007)

[9] Schmitt, K.U., Muser, M.: Investigating reaction times and stopping performance of skiers and snowboarders. Eur. J. Sport Sci. **14**(sup1), S165–S170 (2014).   http://dx.doi.org/10.1080/17461391.2012.666267.   PMID: 24444201

6

Oil Spill Modeling

6.1   Basics of Modeling and Simulation of Oil Spill

Crude oil is a natural, liquid mixture of paraffin, naphthene, and aromatic hydrocarbons. Its main components are paraffin hydrocarbons, sulfur, oxygen, and nitrogen compounds; organo-metallic compounds; and minerals: iron, silicon, vanadium, sodium, and nickel compounds. It is an oily liquid, flammable, brown or black in color. It has a density lower than that of water (within the limits of $0.73-1.04$ $g/cm3$); therefore, it does not mix with it but floats on its surface. Crude oil plays a significant role, in particular, in the chemical and fuel and energy industries. This substance mostly consists of hydrocarbons – with very different molar masses. In addition, it contains heterocyclic and inorganic compounds, which are considered impurities. Individual components occur in different proportions, which results in a large variety of physicochemical properties and is the basis for its classification. The hydrocarbons present in crude oil can be divided as follows [1]:

- n-paraffinic hydrocarbons – unbranched alkanes;

- isoparaffin hydrocarbons – branched alkanes;

- naphthenic hydrocarbons – cycloalkanes, including polycyclics;

- aromatic hydrocarbons mainly benzene and its alkyl derivatives;

- mixed structures – aromatic compounds containing naphthenic structures.

Among the compounds containing heteroatoms are asphaltenes and resins. They are characterized by a significant molar mass. The inorganic compounds in crude oil are mainly water, hydrogen sulfide, salts, and silica.

What is an oil spill? It is the release of a liquid petroleum hydrocarbon into the environment, most often to the aquatic, marine environment, as a result of human activities. One can point out releases from petroleum tankers, drilling rigs/wells, or oil platforms. A small amount of crude oil spilled at sea creates a slick that spreads with sea waves and winds at about 3–4% of the wind speed. Its thickness is the highest at the leak point, and the smallest at the periphery, where it is $0.01-1$ μm. This means that 100 l of oil produces a slick at sea with an average thickness of 0.1 m and an area of 1 km^2. The

DOI: 10.1201/b23388-6

slick disappears spontaneously within 12–24 h as a result of, among others, evaporation, emulsification, dissolution, and absorption by marine flora and fauna. Unfortunately, large spills cannot be absorbed by the ecosystem.

It is estimated that about 3% of the oil produced is released into the environment. Small spills account for 95% of the lost oil, while 5% of the lost oil comes from large spills [2].

One can classify leaks due to:

- causes of formation: anthropogenic or natural spills.

- type of product released: crude oil spills, spills of processed/refined petroleum products.

- amount of released material: small and medium spills are those in which 100–1000 dm^3 are released, and large spills are those over 10 thousand tons.

- elements of a contaminated environment: leakages to soil, seas, inland waters etc.

- leak duration including impulse and chronic leaks.

The consequences of oil spills are very serious: they have a negative impact on the environment, are costly in economic terms, and are often widely reported in the media. The most famous oil spill disasters include Kuwaiti Oil Fires, Oil Lakes, Gulf War (Kuwait 1991), Lakeview Gusher – California (USA 1910), and Deepwater Horizon (USA 2010).

6.1.1   Processes Associated with Oil Spills

The individual processes associated with an oil spill make up a complex system. Taking into account the bottom-up approach, these mechanisms should first be identified and then described in the form of a complex system.

The spread of oil in the sea results from physical, chemical, and biological processes that depend on the properties of the oil, especially composition, density, and viscosity as well as on external conditions such as water temperature, atmospheric pressure, winds, sea currents, and salinity. Among the processes mentioned, the most important are advection, spreading, sedimentation, evaporation, dissolution, emulsification (formation of water-in-oil emulsion), dispersion (formation of an oil-in-water emulsion), photolysis, biodegradation, and interaction with shores. The most important processes are presented in Figure 6.1.

Individual processes have different characteristics, so below are they described in brief.

Evaporation is one of the most important processes to remove oil during a spill. During the first few days, 10% (for heavy or residual oils) up to 75% (for light crudes) of the oil evaporates [3]. As one can easily guess, light

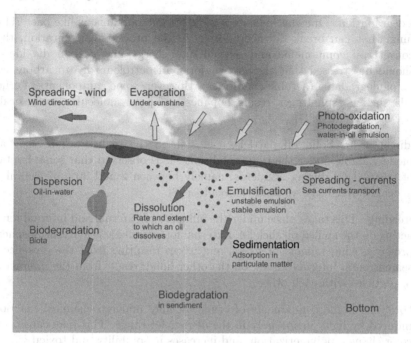

FIGURE 6.1
Oil spill processes.

fractions with low boiling points evaporate the fastest. Thus, as a result of the process, the density and viscosity of the remaining part of the crude oil increase.

Emulsification. During oil spreading, water may enter the oil phase. In this way, a two-phase water-in-oil dispersion system is created. The speed of this process depends on salinity, sea state, and weather conditions. As a result of emulsification, the oil volume, density, and viscosity increase. It is worth emphasizing the fact that resins present in crude oil and acting as emulsifiers stabilize the emulsion [4].

Dissolution. Most oil components are completely insoluble in water. However, some light alkanes and aromatic compounds may dissolve to a small extent [5]. The mechanism that causes the oil to dissolve may be sunlight. Then, in this process, called photo-dissolving, the insoluble components of offshore oil are converted into water-soluble products.

Dispersion. Dispersion is the process by which small drops of oil [6] are drawn into the water column. The condition for this is the separation of the oil located on the surface of the water, into sufficiently small drops. The main factor influencing this process is the wind.

Biodegradation. One can indicate a group of microorganisms like bacteria or fungi that can break down crude oil. In the process of respiration, they convert oil components and oxygen into energy and carbon dioxide. It should be stressed that the vast majority of petroleum hydrocarbons can be biodegradable (aerobic conditions). However, some components of crude oils, such as asphaltenes, resins, hopanes, and polar molecules, are basically not biodegradable [7].

Sedimentation. Solid oil particles can sink to the seabed where they are biodegradable under the right conditions. It is observed that some fraction of released oil during accidents, namely between 2 and 20% of the oil, is allocated over large areas of the seafloor [8].

Spreading. This takes place under the influence of external and internal forces acting on the spilled oil slick [9]. External forces include gravity, atmospheric pressure, wind tangential stress, and forces resulting from the presence of sea currents. Internal forces, on the other hand, result from the interaction of particles with each other.

Photolysis. Some components of crude oil may undergo chemical reactions induced by light – especially in the ultraviolet range. This may cause, e.g., color change, polymerization, and increases in solubility and toxicity.

6.2   Selected Methods of Oil Spill Modeling

An important approach in oil spill modeling uses empirical methods. Conducting empirical tests in laboratory conditions for various types of oils is a valuable source of data. There have been many such studies with oil spill spreading such as by Lehr et al. [10]. The essence of such works was to study the spread of oil on the water surface for different types of oil. On the basis of a series of experimental and analytical works, Fay's papers were created, which describe the key mechanisms involved in oil spreading [11]. Fay divided the decomposition process into three separate phases depending on the driving force and the propagation delay. When the slick is relatively thick, gravity causes the oil to spread sideways; later, the interfacial tension at the edges will be the dominant spreading force. The main decelerating force is initially inertia followed by the viscous resistance of the water. That is why Fay [11] and [12] defined three phases: gravity-inertia, gravity-viscous and surface tension-viscous. The first phase lasts only a few minutes depending on the size of the spot, while the last phase corresponds to the dispersion and marks a separation phase.

Basically, oil spill models are based on two different approaches, namely Eulerian and Lagrangian. The Eulerian approach is based on the mass-momentum conservation equations or alternatively the convection-diffusion equation. The Lagrangian approach with oil spreading uses diffusion equations and simultaneously sea currents and wind mechanisms with diffusion mechanisms. The Lagrangian approach is more suitable for short-term and multi-variant simulations when testing possible spread scenarios, while Euler's approach favors accurate, long-term analyses because these methods are much more computationally expensive [13]. One can point out specialized Lagrangian models such as [14] adapted to surface modeling, [15] vertical mixing, transport and surfacing of particles, and other models such as MED-SLICK I [16] and MEDSLICK II [17] or OpenOil [18]. Examples of Eulerian models are presented in [19] or [20].

An interesting group of grid-based models are models based on Cellular Automata, which, however, differ slightly from the classic Lagrange methods. In Cellular Automata-based models, space is represented by a two- or three-dimensional grid. Each cell contains information about the oil, such as mass, layer thickness, internal condition, and environmental conditions (temperature, pressure, sea currents, and salinity). The change in the internal state of a given cell results from its current state (including internal state and environmental conditions), as well as the states of neighboring cells. On the other hand, the environmental external conditions can be changed independently. The characteristic examples of such an approach are presented in [21] and [22]. One can also identify mixed approach models when the different approaches are combined [9] or [23]. Noteworthy are complex environments in which it is possible to run oil spill simulations, such as ADIOS2 [24]. Due to the multifaceted verification and validation, they are a good source to compare the results of other methods

6.3 Hybrid Approach in Oil Spill Modeling

If we use the discrete method and divide the crude oil into parts, we can quite easily model the advection process, taking into account the influence of sea currents or winds. A significant difficulty, however, is then to calculate the relationship between the individual pieces of oil. This makes it difficult to precisely model oil spreading. A partially effective solution to this problem is the use of the Cellular Automata method. In this case, the movement of oil in a given cell is influenced by the state of intermediate cells. One work [21] presents a comprehensive model of such a system, while its extension along with the algorithm implemented in the FPGA is presented in [22], and the three-dimensional implementation is presented in the work [25]. However, in the case of models based on Cellular Automata, the problem becomes much more complicated in the case of non-homogeneous velocity of the transport medium. Models based solely on Cellular Automata will work great in the absence of advection and assuming uniformity and invariability of external conditions. In [9], we presented a hybrid solution that combines a Lagrangian discrete particle algorithm with the Cellular Automata approach. This will allow both to model advection and to take into account the variability of external conditions. Below I present the basic assumptions of this model with some comments.

6.3.1 Basic Elements of the Model

The spreading process is based on the Fay model [11], for which a framework based on the discrete division of space was proposed. The oil slick was broken up into small particles which were named Oil Particles (OPs). OPs have specific parameters such as mass, density, or composition. The sea and land are divided by a square grid. OPs are assigned to this grid, then move according to the velocity field corresponding to the influence of sea currents or wind. In addition, individual OPs are affected by processes such as emulsification, evaporation, or dispersion. Of course, the operation of these processes depends on the external conditions to which the cells are subject. The clamp that binds the operation of the entire model is CA, which describes the dynamics of the OPs movement.

The entire simulation is carried out in the Cartesian coordinate system, and each cell represents water or land. In the model, we take into account both external and internal variables, which are, respectively:

CEV – Cell External Variables, among which we can distinguish external conditions such as temperature, winds, and sea currents;

CIV – Cell Internal Variables, among which we can distinguish thickness of the oil layer, water content, and so on.

Oil is represented by, mentioned before, discrete Oil Particles. OPs are characterized by actual coordinates and assigned to individual grid cells: squares with coordinates $x \in [ja, (j+1)a$ and $y \in [ia, (i+1a)]$ are assigned to the cell with i, j indexes. Their movement is associated with advection and spreading. Their state can be updated according to changing parameters such as volume, water content, mass, and rates of dispersion and evaporation. These properties are described as OPS, i.e., Oil Point State. The scheme is presented in Figure 6.2.

6.3.2 Algorithm of the Hybrid Oil Spill Model

The hybrid simulation is performed in discrete time steps. The main algorithm is presented in Figure 6.3.

The first step of the algorithm is to set the input data, including oil composition, and parameters and assign terrain topography, including water and

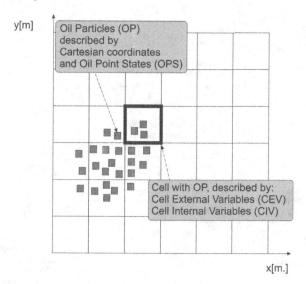

FIGURE 6.2
Hybrid approach in oil spill modeling: Cells of Cellular Automata with Oil
Point States (OPS) including Oil Particles.

land, to particular cells of the simulation (Table 6.1). The next step is to set
Cell External Variables (CEV) and length of time step. Next, it should be decided if we add oil with mass m to particular cells (i, j). If we add the oil, we
should divide it into n Oil Points (OPS) $(n = m/m_k)$ and select coordinates
for each OP.

6.4   Component Processes in the Spreading of Oil Spills

Several component processes can be identified that determine the spread of an
oil slick on the surface of the sea. In the first step, for the identified processes,
we should indicate the appropriate rules and equations related to their essence,
and then combine the operation of these processes into one algorithm. This
algorithm was described in the previous section, and in the current section,
attention should be paid to specific processes [9]. This is a classic example
of system emergence, i.e., it is based on several phenomena with relatively
simple rules, and only the combination of these phenomena manifests itself in
the overall picture of the system in the form of oil slick spreading.

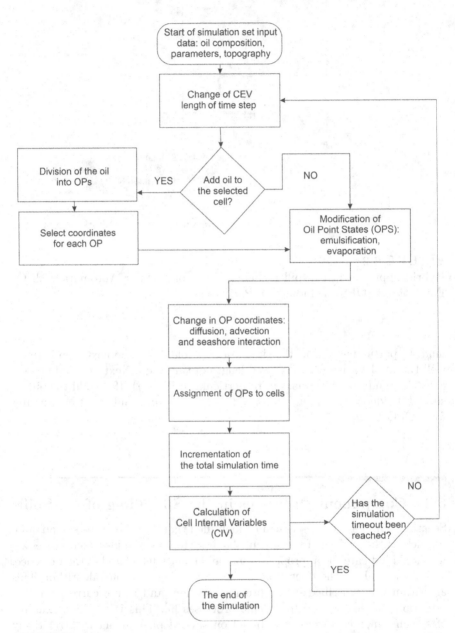

FIGURE 6.3
Algorithm of the hybrid model.

TABLE 6.1
Scheme of Data Flow in the Simulation.

Stage	Description
Initialization of simulation	Define terrain topography. Define oil parameters: composition, density, viscosity, and surface tension, as well as mass value of a piece of oil.
Update value of CEV and time step length	Update CEV (Cell External Variables) in each time step. Change time step if it's profitable.
Add oil to some cells	Define places of oil leaks to one or multiply source. Add oil to selected cells n OPs.
Modify OPS for each OP	Update the next state OPS due to particular processes such as evaporation, emulsification, dispersion, updates regarding viscosity, and density.
Update OP coordinates	In consecutive time steps, changes in OP coordinates are foreseen. They are carried out due to advection, diffusion, and seashore interaction.
Allocate OPs to cells	In this step, part of the OP can be transferred to other cells. From a technological point of view, a list with aggregated OPs is created.
Simulation timer update	In this step, the indication of the simulation clock is increased in accordance with the adopted time step.
Calculation of CIV	CIV (Cell Internal Variables) are calculated due to the list of OPs assigned to the cell for each cell. The results of the function are the oil states at a current time and specific surface area.
The end of the simulation	Stopping the simulation clock and terminating the algorithm after reaching the assumed number of simulations or other stopping condition.

6.4.1 Advection

Advection means the lifting of a substance by a flowing fluid in such a way that the velocity of the lifted substance is equal to the velocity of the flowing fluid. Thus, advection means, in practice, the mechanism of transport of a substance through a fluid as a result of bulk (mass) motion of the fluid.

The mechanism of advection is bound closely with the OP motion using a uniform linear approximation – we proposed such a mechanism in [9]. The characteristics of the OP motion, especially the velocity, contain the combined influence of wind and sea currents. Thus, we can write the OP displacement equation as follows taking into account the kth iteration in the i, j cell:

$$\Delta \mathbf{r}_k = \alpha \mathbf{v}_k^{current}(ij) + \beta \mathbf{v}_k^{wind}(ij)\Delta t_k \qquad (6.1)$$

where $\mathbf{v}_k^{current}(ij)$ and $\mathbf{v}_k^{wind}(ij)$ represent vectors of current and wind velocities specified in the kth iteration in the i,j cell, Δt_k is the defined time step. Parameter values α and β equal respectively to 1.1 and 3% were adopted in accordance with [26] and [27], respectively. The adopted value of β is valid for external conditions, when the sea is calm. In conditions where there is a large wave of the sea surface or Langmuir cells are present, spreading due to surface tension becomes negligible which was confirmed in the works [28] and [29].

6.4.2   Spreading

At the beginning, what is the spreading process in the practice of modeling the dynamics of oil on the sea surface? The answer is quite simple: it is a process of increasing the surface of the oil slick while reducing its thickness. In our case, we should therefore move the OP accordingly. Unlike the process of advection, it is necessary to consider the correlation between OPs because the spreading motion of a single OP is dependent on the position of other OPs. In our model, we did it analogously with the diffusion process, although it should be emphasized that diffusion is a different process; however, it can serve only as an analogy, which has been confirmed by research [30] and [31]. We adapted in [9] a method using Cellular Automata with interactions among cells with diffusion-induced mass flow calculated separately for each pair of adjacent cells. For the adjacent cells, the flowing mass Δm is calculated according to the following formula taking into account a one-dimensional case:

$$\Delta m = \frac{1}{2}(m_{i+1} - m_i)\left(1 - exp\left(-2\frac{D}{\Delta x^2}\Delta t\right)\right) \qquad (6.2)$$

where Δx is length of the cell, Δt is the time step, and the mass of cell i is described as m_i.

Taking into account two-dimensional Cellular Automata, we use another formula dedicated for a von Neumann neighborhood:

1. $u_{i1}/u_{i2}, u_{i3}/u_{i4}, u_{i5}/u_{i6}$
2. $u_{i0}/u_{i1}, u_{i2}/u_{i3}, u_{i4}/u_{i5}$
3. $u_{1j}/u_{2j}, u_{3j}/u_{4j}, u_{5j}/u_{6j}$
4. $u_{0j}/u_{1j}, u_{2j}/u_{3j}, u_{4j}/u_{5j}$

Masses of cells are taken into account during calculations of the flow of oil among adjacent cells (6.2). It should be stressed that the total mass of particular cells is the sum of all OPs in the region of interest. The dynamics of the Δm mass flow is related to changes in the number of OPs.

If the thickness of the oil film assigned to a given cell is greater than the final thickness, which can be estimated by the following formula $\delta_{min} = 10^{-5}V_0^{1/4}$, where δ_{min} is the final layer thickness $[m]$ and V_0 is initial value m^3, we can use the following procedure presented in Figure 6.4.

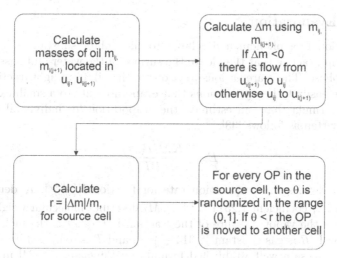

FIGURE 6.4
Algorithm of spreading process.

Regarding the spreading diffusion coefficient D, we take into account Fay's spreading theory [11] with three phases:

gravity-inertial – dominant in the first several dozen minutes

gravity-viscous – most important in the time range from one hour to seven days

viscous-surface – most important one week after the beginning of the leak

Taking into account the second phase, we can calculate slick area (A) using the formula by [32].

$$A = 0.98^2 \pi \left(\frac{V^2 g \Delta}{\nu_w^{1/2}} \right)^{1/3} t^{1/2} \qquad (6.3)$$

where V is oil volume, g means gravitational acceleration, Δ is the ratio of the density difference between water and oil to the density of water, ν_w is kinematic viscosity of sea water, and t represents time calculated from the beginning of the leak.

We can solve the diffusion equation (1D) that is a Gaussian function with the standard deviation σ using the formula $\sigma = \sqrt{2Dt}$ and next, taking into account the calculated A (the slick area), we can define $D = \frac{0.48}{n^2} (\frac{V^2 g \Delta}{\nu_w^{1/2}})^{1/3} t^{-1/2}$ taking into account the propagating wave method. And next, we calculate D for all pairs of cells and particular time steps [9].

6.4.3 Evaporation

Evaporation is a phenomenon related to the lighter substances in the oil, meaning in practice that they leave the surface of the water and pass into the gaseous phase. There are various fractions in the oil, from light fractions that evaporate easily to heavy fractions that evaporate only to a small extent. An effective formula that can estimate the evaporation for individual fractions can be written as follows [33]:

$$E_I = \frac{K M_I P_{0I} x_I}{RT} \tag{6.4}$$

where E_I defines the evaporation rate for fraction I $[\frac{kg}{m^2 \cdot s}]$, K denotes the mass transfer coefficient $1.25 \cdot 10^{-3}$ $[\frac{m}{s}]$, M_I describes molecular weight, $[\frac{kg}{mol}]$, P_{0I} defines the vapor pressure of the fraction I $[Pa]$, x_I is the mole fraction of fraction I, R is gas constant $[8.314 \frac{J}{mol \cdot K}]$, and T is temperature $[K]$.

One can use a well-established formula by Fingas et al. [34] in order to calculate vapor pressure:

$$P_{0I} = 1000 \cdot exp\left(-(4.4 + lnT_b)\left(1.803\left(\frac{T_{bI}}{T} - 1\right) - 0.803 ln\left(\frac{T_{bI}}{T}\right)\right)\right) \tag{6.5}$$

Next, we calculate the molar mass of component I using an equation by Win [35]:

$$M_I = 2.410 \cdot 10^{-6}\left(T_{bI}^{2.847}\left(\frac{\rho_0}{\rho_{w(4^\circ C)}}\right)^{-2.130}\right) \tag{6.6}$$

where $\rho_{w(4^\circ C)}$ is water density at $4^\circ C$ and ρ_0 is oil density.

In this situation, x_I denotes the mole fraction. We determine it taking into account the mass fractions w_I and the molar mass M_J:

$$x_I = \frac{w_I/M_I}{\sum_{J=1}^{n} w_J/M_J} \tag{6.7}$$

Finally we take the individual equations together, namely mass for each fraction (Δm_I), evaporation process in time steps Δt, Eq. 6.4, Δt, and area A and we calculate the final equation for each fraction (component) for all OPs:

$$\Delta m_I = \frac{K M_I P_{0I} x_I}{RT} A \Delta t \tag{6.8}$$

6.4.4 Emulsification

Emulsification consists in the fact that drops of water under the influence of waves can penetrate into the oil and then a water-in-oil emulsion is formed. It can be modeled from the following formula [36]:

$$\frac{dY}{dt} = K_Y (v^{wind} + 1)^2 \left(1 - \frac{Y}{C}\right) \tag{6.9}$$

where K_Y is represented as $2.0 \cdot 10^{-6}$, Y is the content of water in the emulsion, v^{wind} is wind speed (m/s), and C is max content of water in the water-in-oil emulsion.

In order to calculate the change in emulsification rate during a time step Δt in all OPs, it is profitable to use a formula from [9]:

$$\Delta Y_k = 2.0 \cdot 10^{-6}(v^{wind} + 1)^2 \left(1 - \frac{Y_k}{C}\right)\Delta t. \qquad (6.10)$$

Parameter v^{wind} describes the wind connected with a cell wherein the considered OP is located.

6.4.5 Changes in the Oil Density – Evaporation and Emulsification

In general, the density of the emulsion (ρ_e) is described as a weighted mean of the initial density of oil (ρ_0) and the density of water (ρ_w). Another important issue is the percentage of emulsification:

$$\rho_e = (1 - Y)\rho_0 + Y\rho_w. \qquad (6.11)$$

On the other hand, evaporation can be described as [26]:

$$\rho = (0.6\rho_0 - 340)F + \rho_0. \qquad (6.12)$$

The final equation takes into account the density of the emulsion as a function of the progress of evaporation and emulsification [9]:

$$\rho_e = (1 - Y)((0.6\rho_0 - 340)F + \rho_0) + Y\rho_w. \qquad (6.13)$$

Finally, equation 6.13 is valid for all OPs for a particular time step in order to actualize the density of emulsion (in an OP).

6.4.6 Natural Dispersion

During natural dispersion, small droplets of oil are transferred into the water column. Such a mechanism is induced by waves and has a significant effect on oil spreading/removing [37].

$$D = D_a D_b, \qquad (6.14)$$

where D_a is the fraction of oil dispersed per hour and D_b is dispersed oil which does not return to the surface. One can use the following equations in order to calculate the parameters:

$$D_a = 0.11(v^{wind} + 1)^2 \qquad (6.15)$$

$$D_b = \frac{1}{1 + 50\sqrt{\mu \delta s_t}} \qquad (6.16)$$

where v^{wind} is speed of wind $[m/s]$, μ is dynamic viscosity $[cP]$, δ is slick thickness $[cm]$, and s_t is oil-water interfacial tension $[dyna/cm]$.

The change in s_t can be expressed as [38]:

$$s_t = s_{t0}(1 + F) \qquad (6.17)$$

where s_{t0} is initial interfacial tension and F is the fraction of evaporated oil.

Taking into account the previous equations, it is right to use the following formula:

$$\Delta m_{dysp} = m \cdot D_a D_b / 3600 \cdot \Delta t \qquad (6.18)$$

where m is the current oil mass assigned to the OP and Δm_{dysp} is oil mass that was removed by dispersion.

6.4.7   Viscosity of Oil as a Dynamic Process

The viscosity of the oil increases significantly due to the processes of evaporation and emulsification.

$$\frac{d\mu}{dt} = C_2 \mu \frac{dF}{dt} + \frac{2.5\mu}{(1 - CY)^2} \frac{dY}{dt} \qquad (6.19)$$

where F is the fraction of evaporated oil, Y describes the content of water in emulsion, C denotes the maximum value of content of water in emulsion, and C_2 is a type of oil parameter. Finally, in [9] we proposed the following formula:

$$\Delta\mu = C_2 \mu \Delta F + \frac{2.5\mu \Delta Y}{(1 - CY)^2} \qquad (6.20)$$

6.4.8   Interaction with the Seashore

During a spill, the oil can reach the shoreline and interact with different types of beaches, boulders, rocks, and so on. This causes erosion and pollution, and some of the material is returned to the water by wave action. It can be defined using first-order kinetics with a proportional rate of movement of oil from land to sea and sea to land [39].

$$\frac{dm}{dt} = -km \qquad (6.21)$$

where k is a proportionality constant determined according to the type of coast.

Half-decay time is also an important concept and can be denoted as $k = \frac{ln(2)}{t_{1/2}}$. Thus, finally we can formulate the equation including the change in oil mass contained in the shoreline cell which results from a return to the sea [9] in the time step Δt:

$$\Delta m = -\frac{ln(2)}{t_{1/2}} m \Delta t \qquad (6.22)$$

Similar to the spreading process, oil fluctuation is simulated by moving the OP from the land cell to the adjacent water cell with the probability given by the ratio $|\Delta m|/m$.

6.5 Simulation of Oil Spills

A computer simulation was created based on the proposed hybrid model [9]. We have taken into account crude oil of the Statfjord type. The following parameters have been taken into account:

Cell size $-$ $10, 20$, and $50\ m$

No. of rows $-$ 150

No. of cols $-$ 150

Initial oil mass $-$ $100\ t$

Initial area $-$ $50000\ m^2$

Minimal oil thickness δ_{min} $-$ $0.03\ mm$

Initial shape of the oil slick $-$ circular shape

Time step $-$ $20, 50, 100, 200, 300$, and $600\ s$

Salinity $-$ $32\ ppt$

Oil density $15^{\circ}C$ $-$ $835\ kg/m^3$

Propagation factor $-$ 3

Surface tension $dyne/s$ $-$ $30\ dyne/s$

C constant $-$ 0.7

Total time $-$ $200\ h$

Initial oil mass in OP $-$ $1, 2, 5, 10, 20$, and $50\ kg$

An important stage of oil spill simulation on the basis of the discrete method is to check the effect of selection of cell size and time step length. These parameters include important spatial, matter, and time aspects of the simulation. A simple rule applies: the larger the cell, the faster the evaporation rate. Analogically, the mass of a single OP should be small enough to have more than one OP in a given cell with minimal oil thickness. An extensive analysis related to the calibration procedures and mesh size selection is described in our article [9].

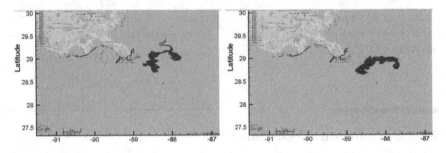

FIGURE 6.5
The Deepwater Horizon oil spill: the oil imprint on the water surface – (left) real data from the DWH oil spill [41–43] – 25 April 2010 versus the presented model (right) – a sketch with visible impact on the waterfront area.

6.5.1   An Example – Deepwater Horizon 2010

The explosion on the Deepwater Horizon oil platform located in the Gulf of Mexico occurred on 20 April 2010. The cause was a natural gas explosion, which caused a fire, damage to the platform, and, consequently, a massive oil leak – the largest oil spill in history. The rig capsized and sank on the morning of April 22 [40]. We prepared a test of the proposed hybrid algorithms taking into account the following parameters: cell size 200 m, time step 1200 s, and initial mass of an OP 50 kg. We assumed that the volume of oil escaping was 15000 barrels per day (2285000 l per day). We also applied wind data, obtained through the application of drifters, made available to us by Dr Yonggang Liu from Ocean Circulation Group and ocean currents data from Goods service.

The results of the comparison are presented in Figure 6.5:

The aim of the simulated scenario was to approximately demonstrate that the model's outcomes, namely oil imprint on the water surface, resemble reality. The results obtained suggest that the proposed hybrid model correctly reproduces advection as well as spreading processes [9]. The proposed hybrid model, unlike many available models, takes into account advection in predicting chemical and physical properties. It should be stressed that advection depends on wind and sea currents. It should be emphasized that wind and temperature primarily affect the properties studied in the previous chapters. Hence, in the case of uniform wind and temperature fields, advection should not have a significant impact on the considered processes. We confirmed this conclusion by running several simulations with and without advection – the observed differences have been insignificant.

6.6   Verification and Validation

Finally, in the simulation, we adopted the following parameters: cell size 20 m, mass of OP 5 kg, and time step 20 s (Figure 6.6). For comparative purposes, we

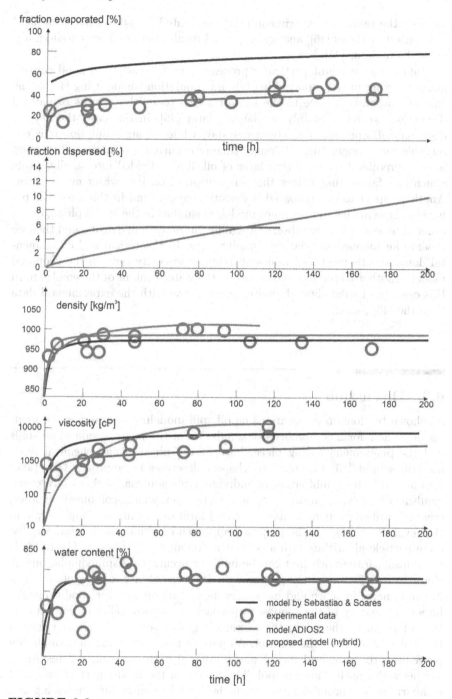

FIGURE 6.6
Comparison of different characteristics for: ADIOS2, experimental data, Sebastiao & Soares model, and proposed hybrid model.

adopted the results of experimental data presented in [44], results from hand calculation methods [36], and we compared results to data from a well-known oil spill simulator [45].

Taking into account particular processes, we have achieved good convergence to experiments reported in [44] and simulations made using [45] in the case of evaporation. Due to the lack of access to reliable results of natural dispersion, we relied mainly on the simulator [45]. In this case, the natural dispersion disappears after about one day, while in our simulation it is observable for a longer time. A longer time of occurrence of natural dispersion is more credible because a thin layer of oil film is divided into smaller spots which is a factor that makes the penetration of oil into water much easier. Another aspect to be compared is density changes, and in this case, the behavior of the model and reference models is similar: in the initial phase, of the order of several hours, we observe a significant increase in density, and then we observe an increase of relatively small values. In theoretical and experimental data, we observe lower values of dynamic viscosity than in the proposed model. Another factor to be compared is the water content of the emulsion. In this case, the model showed greater convergence with the experimental data than the [45] model.

6.7   Discussion

As shown by domain publications on oil spill modeling, comprehensive models that allow for a comprehensive simulation of the phenomenon of oil spills and the phenomena taking place, both at the physical and chemical level, are still sought [13, 15, 20]. This chapter describes an approach that takes into account the combination of individual phenomena, such as advection, emulsification, evaporation, or natural dispersion, which, combined together, create the phenomenon of emergence and form one common complex system that evolves over time. The proposed approach combines the Lagrangian discrete particle algorithm with a cellular automaton, Section 6.2. The result is a promising framework that can be used for accurate oil spill simulations. A characteristic feature of the proposed model is the ability to take into account inhomogeneity in space and instability depending on weather conditions. An important feature of the proposed approach is the possibility of determining the condition of the oil in the average – global sense, as well as referring to local fragments of the oil film. As part of the verification and validation procedure, the proposed model was compared with experimental results as well as with another known tool. The results of the model performance and comparisons are promising, although the model requires further testing and development.

Bibliography

[1] Sliwka, E.: Group composition of oil fractions analysis by column chromatography. Materials of the Wrocław University of Technology (2010)

[2] Surygała, J., Śliwka E. Oil spills. Journal of Chemical Industry - Poland 78(9), 323–325 (1999)

[3] Fingas, M.F.: The evaporation of oil spills: Development and implementation of new prediction methodology. Int. Oil Spill Conf. Proc. **1999**(1), 281–287 (1999). https://doi.org/10.7901/2169-3358-1999-1-281

[4] Wang, S., Shen, Y., Zheng, Y.: Two-dimensional numerical simulation for transport and fate of oil spills in seas. Ocean Eng. **32**(13), 1556–1571 (2005). https://doi.org/10.1016/j.oceaneng.2004.12.010. https://www.sciencedirect.com/science/article/pii/S0029801805000454

[5] Hassanshahian, M., Cappello, S.: Crude oil biodegradation in the marine environments. In: R. Chamy, F. Rosenkranz (eds.) Biodegradation, chap. 5. IntechOpen, Rijeka (2013). https://doi.org/10.5772/55554

[6] Liu, Z., Callies, U.: A probabilistic model of decision making regarding the use of chemical dispersants to combat oil spills in the German bight. Water Res. **169**, 115–196 (2020). https://doi.org/10.1016/j.watres.2019.115196. https://www.sciencedirect.com/science/article/pii/S0043135419309704

[7] Atlas, R.M., Hazen, T.C.: Oil biodegradation and bioremediation: A tale of the two worst spills in U.S. history. Environ. Sci. Technol. **45**(16), 6709–6715 (2011). https://doi.org/10.1021/es2013227. PMID: 21699212

[8] Passow, U., Stout, S.A.: Character and sedimentation of "lingering" Macondo oil to the deep-sea after the Deepwater Horizon oil spill. Mar. Chem. **218**, 103, 733 (2020). https://doi.org/10.1016/j.marchem.2019.103733. https://www.sciencedirect.com/science/article/pii/S0304420319302403

[9] Gług, M., Wąs, J.: Modeling of oil spill spreading disasters using combination of Langrangian discrete particle algorithm with cellular automata approach. Ocean Eng. **156**, 396–405 (2018). https://doi.org/10.1016/j.oceaneng.2018.01.029. https://www.sciencedirect.com/science/article/pii/S0029801818300295

[10] Lehr, W., Cekirge, H., Fraga, R., Belen, M.: Empirical studies of the spreading of oil spills. Oil Petr. Pollut. **2**(1), 7–11 (1984). https://doi.org/10.1016/S0143-7127(84)90637-9. https://www.sciencedirect.com/science/article/pii/S0143712784906379

[11] Fay, J.: Physical processes in the spread of oil on a water surface. Annu. Rev. Fluid Mech., 4(1), 341–368 (1972). https://doi.org/10.1146/annurev.fl.04.010172.002013

[12] Hoult, D.P.: Oil spreading on the sea. Annu. Rev. Fluid Mech. 4(1), 341–368 (1972). https://doi.org/10.1146/annurev.fl.04.010172.002013

[13] Keramea, P., Spanoudaki, K., Zodiatis, G., Gikas, G., Sylaios, G.: Oil spill modeling: A critical review on current trends, perspectives, and challenges. J. Mar. Sci. Eng. 9(2) (2021). https://doi.org/10.3390/jmse9020181. https://www.mdpi.com/2077-1312/9/2/181

[14] Brovchenko, I., Maderich, V.: Numerical Lagrangian method for the modelling of the surface oil slick. Appl Hydromech 4(76), 23–31 (2002)

[15] Nordam, T., Kristiansen, R., Nepstad, R., Röhrs, J.: Numerical analysis of boundary conditions in a Lagrangian particle model for vertical mixing, transport and surfacing of buoyant particles in the water column. Ocean Model. **136**, 107–119 (2019). https://doi.org/10.1016/j.ocemod.2019.03.003. https://www.sciencedirect.com/science/article/pii/S1463500319300319

[16] Lardner, R., Zodiatis, G., Hayes, D., Pinardi, N.: Application of the MEDSLIK oil spill model to the Lebanese spill of July 2006. European Group of Experts on satellite monitoring of sea based oil pollution, European Communities ISSN pp. 1018–5593 (2006)

[17] De Dominicis, M., Pinardi, N., Zodiatis, G., Lardner, R.: MEDSLIK-II, a Lagrangian marine surface oil spill model for short-term forecasting – part 1: Theory. Geosci. Model Dev. **6**, 1851–1869 (2013). https://doi.org/10.5194/gmd-6-1851-2013

[18] Röhrs, J., Dagestad, K.F., Asbjørnsen, H., Nordam, T., Skancke, J., Jones, C.E., Brekke, C.: The effect of vertical mixing on the horizontal drift of oil spills. Ocean Sci. **14**(6), 1581–1601 (2018). https://doi.org/10.5194/os-14-1581-2018. https://os.copernicus.org/articles/14/1581/2018/

[19] Nagheeby, M., Kolahdoozan, M.: Numerical modeling of two-phase fluid flow and oil slick transport in estuarine water. Int. J. Environ. Sci. Technol. **7**, 771–784 (2010)

[20] Barker, C.H., Kourafalou, V.H., Beegle-Krause, C., Boufadel, M., Bourassa, M.A., Buschang, S.G., Androulidakis, Y., Chassignet, E.P., Dagestad, K.F., Danmeier, D.G., et al.: Progress in operational modeling in support of oil spill response. J. Mar. Sci. Eng. **8**(9), 668 (2020)

[21] Karafyllidis, I.: A model for the prediction of oil slick movement and spreading using cellular automata. Environ. Int.

23(6), 839–850 (1997). https://doi.org/10.1016/S0160-4120(97)00096-2. https://www.sciencedirect.com/science/article/pii/S0160412097000962

[22] Rusinovic, Z., Bogunovic, N.: Cellular automata based model for the prediction of oil slicks behavior. In: 28th International Conference on Information Technology Interfaces, pp. 569–574 (2006). https://doi.org/10.1109/ITI.2006.1708543

[23] Fraga, B., Stoesser, T., Lai, C.C., Socolofsky, S.A.: A LES-based Eulerian–Lagrangian approach to predict the dynamics of bubble plumes. Ocean Model. **97**, 27–36 (2016)

[24] Lehr, W., Jones, R., Evans, M., Simecek-Beatty, D., Overstreet, R.: Revisions of the adios oil spill model. Environ. Model. Softw. **17**(2), 189–197 (2002)

[25] Vourkas I., Sirakoulis G.: FPGA implementation of a cellular automata-based algorithm for the prediction of oil slick spreading. In: Proceedings of the 19th IEEE International Conference on Electronics, Circuits, and Systems (ICECS2012), pp. 1–4. IEEE, Piscataway, NJ

[26] Wang, S., Shen, Y., Zheng, Y.: Two-dimensional numerical simulation for transport and fate of oil spills in seas. Ocean Eng. **32**(13), 1556–1571 (2005)

[27] Boufadel, M.C., Abdollahi-Nasab, A., Geng, X., Galt, J., Torlapati, J.: Simulation of the landfall of the Deepwater Horizon oil on the shorelines of the Gulf of Mexico. Environ. Sci. Technol. **48**(16), 9496–9505 (2014). http://dx.doi.org/10.1021/es5012862. PMID: 25068902

[28] Boufadel, M.C., Bechtel, R.D., Weaver, J.: The movement of oil under non-breaking waves. Mar. Pollut. Bull. **52**(9), 1056 – 1065 (2006). https://doi.org/10.1016/j.marpolbul.2006.01.012. http://www.sciencedirect.com/science/article/pii/S0025326X06000336

[29] Geng, X., Boufadel, M.C., Ozgokmen, T., King, T., Lee, K., Lu, Y., Zhao, L.: Oil droplets transport due to irregular waves: Development of large-scale spreading coefficients. Mar. Pollut. Bull. **104**(1), 279–289 (2016). https://doi.org/10.1016/j.marpolbul.2016.01.007. URL http://www.sciencedirect.com/science/article/pii/S0025326X16300078

[30] Ao-Ieong, E., Chang, A., Gu, S.: Modeling the BP oil spill of 2010: A simplified model of oil diffusion in water (2012). https://isn.ucsd.edu/courses/beng221/problems/2012/BENG221_Project%20-%20Ao-Ieong%20Change%20Gu.pdf

[31] Vick, B.: Multi-physics modeling using cellular automata. Complex Syst **17**(1/2), 65–78 (2007)

[32] Wang, X., Campbell, J.R., Ditmars, J.D.: Computer modeling of oil drift and spreading in Delaware Bay. Department of Civil Engineering and College of Marine Studies, University of Delaware, Newark, DE (1976)

[33] Tkalin, A.: Evaporation of petroleum hydrocarbons from films on a smooth sea surface. Oceanology ONLGAE **26**(4) (1986)

[34] Fingas, M.: Modeling oil and petroleum evaporation. J. Pet. Sci. Res. 104–115 (2013)

[35] Winn, F.: Physical properties by nomogram. Petroleum Refiner **36**(2), 157–159 (1957)

[36] Sebastiao, P., Guedes Soares, C.: Modeling the fate of oil spills at sea. Spill Sci. Technol. Bull. **2**(2), 121–131 (1995)

[37] Reed, M.: The physical fates component of the natural resource damage assessment model system. Oil and Chemical Pollution **5**(2), 99–123 (1989)

[38] Mackay, D., Arnot, J.A.: The application of fugacity and activity to simulating the environmental fate of organic contaminants. J. Chem. Eng. Data **56**(4), 1348–1355 (2011). http://doi.org/10.1021/je101158y 2011

[39] Shen, H.T., Yapa, P.D., Petroski, M.E.: A simulation model for oil slick transport in lakes. Water Resour. Res. **23**(10), 1949–1957 (1987)

[40] Pallardy, R.: Deepwater Horizon oil spill of 2010. Encyclopedia Britannica.com. (2015) www.britannica.com/event/Deepwater-Horizon-oil-spill-of-2010

[41] Liu, Y., Weisberg, R.H., Vignudelli, S., Mitchum, G.T.: Evaluation of altimetry-derived surface current products using Lagrangian drifter trajectories in the eastern Gulf of Mexico. J. Geophys. Res. Oceans **119**(5), 2827–2842 (2014). http://dx.doi.org/10.1002/2013JC009710

[42] Liu, Y., Weisberg, R.H.: Evaluation of trajectory modeling in different dynamic regions using normalized cumulative Lagrangian separation. J. Geophys. Res. Oceans **116**(C9), n/a–n/a (2011). http://dx.doi.org/10.1029/2010JC006837. C09013

[43] Liu, Y., Weisberg, R.H., Hu, C., Zheng, L.: Tracking the Deepwater Horizon oil spill: A modeling perspective. Eos **92**(6), 45–46 (2011). http://dx.doi.org/10.1029/2011EO060001

[44] Buchanan, I., Hurford, N.: Methods for predicting the physical changes in oil spilt at sea. Oil and Chem. Pol. **4**(4), 311–328 (1988)

[45] Automated data inquiry for oil spills (ADIOS) (2016). http://response.restoration.noaa.gov/ADIOS

7

Summary

This book covers a number of distinctive complex systems. Some of them concern the movement of intelligent particles (pedestrian traffic, movement of downhill skiers on a slope or road traffic), while some refer to complex systems occurring in nature like the spread of oil on the sea surface.

The adopted models and implementations resulted from the applications and current needs as well as the possibilities of validation and verification. I believe that openness to various modeling methods is justified and the use of particular modeling and simulation methods depends on what we want to achieve.

One should also bear in mind the limitations associated with the use of the cellular automaton paradigm. A significant limitation is the discretization of time and space. One should be aware that space and time will be affected by inaccuracies, which should be taken into account both when creating the model itself and the validation and verification procedures.

In individual chapters, different modeling methods were chosen depending on the needs: in the case of pedestrians, it was an agent-based approach based on Cellular Automata, in the case of skiers an agent-based approach, but based on a continuous force model, the driver simulator was based on the modification of the Nagel-Schreckenberg cell model, while in the case of oil spill modeling, we relied on the Lagrange approach with Cellular Automata.

For large-scale crowd models, simulator performance is key, hence the discretization of time and space, and a relatively simple representation of a pedestrian allows for high performance. For skiers, the representation in the form of a cellular automaton is insufficient because their movement is smooth and only a continuous approach gives a good result to estimate the risk of a collision. Of course, it is possible to imagine the situation that a skier model based on a cellular automaton would be used for rough safety estimates. In this case, we proposed a continuous approach using the Social Force Model, taking into account the specificity of the physics of the skier's movement. However, important elements of these models are the field of view, skiers' skills, and the safety zones around the skier, which make up the agent-based characteristics of the system. This model also works very effectively and realistically.

In the case of road traffic, the decisive factor in choosing this methodology based on the extended Na-Sch model was the efficiency of the method with the simultaneous addition of many important elements: several lanes taking into account the lane change maneuver, traffic lights, joining the traffic, etc.

DOI: 10.1201/b23388-7

In the chapters devoted to the movement of intelligent particles, i.e., the dynamics of pedestrians, skiers, and drivers, an Agent-Based Modeling approach in which the particle is presented as an agent is a very important element. In our projects, we considered a number of features, properties of agents. It is possible to differentiate the types of behavior: different profiles of people, level of advancement (e.g. skiing skills or driving skills), and willingness to cooperate or compete with other agents. It is also possible to globally define a situation where a community of agents may be subject to emotions or similar behavior. For example, during evacuation: competitive evacuation, panic, cooperative evacuation, and stampede.

In the case of some crowd models, such as those presented in the chapters concerning crowds and drivers (Chapters 3 and 4), non-homogeneous and Asynchronous Cellular Automata were a good foundation for the operation of the model. Additionally, for the purpose of obtaining realistic behaviors, an agent-based mechanism was introduced, in which each entity in the simulation is represented by an agent. This gives a realistic effect in the phenomenon of emergence, where we observe that pedestrians are subject to more or less fluctuations, which is visible in the flow statistics, or we see different types of trajectories in the movement of skiers. This is a good example where the distinction between different types of behavior is visible in the system image (the phenomenon of emergence in complex systems). The model is not yet very complicated in terms of rules, and at the same time, the introduction of agent rules gives a specific emergence effect (skiers' trajectories, matrix of pedestrians visits, and trajectories).

The agent-based approach to modeling also shows the phenomenon of self-organization, where the ordering of structures for specific classes of situations is visible in all systems.

For the oil spill, it was crucial to find an efficient oil flow model and take into account the most important factors while maintaining high efficiency.

The presented models propose certain directions of development, taking into account the specific needs discussed above. More than 20 years after the publication of Wolfram's *The New Kind of Science*, my work with my colleagues has shown that Cellular Automata are indeed an important technology in modeling dependencies and collective aspects in complex systems. At the moment, however, there is no reason to claim that they have superseded other modeling methods. They are often an important contribution or fragment in modeling the effective modeling of these systems.

The work to date has shown that homogeneous and asynchronous automata are of particular practical importance and that the hybrid method, in which it is combined with other methods, works best in particular.

Index

Advanced Driver Assistance
    Systems, 51
advection, 97
agent representation, 24
agent systems, 31
Agent-Based Modeling, 24
Asynchronous Cellular
    Automata, 22

behavior of crowd, 27
biodegradation of oil, 92
boundary conditions, 12

Cell External Variables, 94
Cell Internal Variables, 94
Cellular Automata, 11
cellular automaton, 11
classification of Cellular
    Automata, 14
competitive evacuation, 47
complex collective system, 1
complex system, 1
crowd classification, 27

Deepwater Horizon disaster, 104
dispersion of oil, 91
dissolution of oil, 91

Elementary Cellular
    Automata, 12
emergence, 1
emulsification of oil, 91
evaporation of oil, 91

FHP method, 23
fundamental diagram, 47

Game of Life, 16

Helbing-Molnár-Farkas-Vicsek
    (HMFV) model, 33
HPP method, 23
hybrid approach in oil spill modeling,
    93

interaction strength, 33

Lagrangian discrete particle
    algorithm, 94
Langton's Ant, 17
large room evacuation, 40
Lattice Boltzmann algorithm, 24
Lattice Gas Automata, 22
Leading head model, 54

macroscopic approach in crowd
    dynamics, 29
Margolus neighborhood, 20
microscopic approach in crowd
    dynamics, 31
model assessment, 2
Moore neighborhood, 20

Nagel-Schreckenberg model, 52
neighbor repulsion forces, 75
non-competitive evacuation, 47
non-homogeneous Cellular
    Automata, 22

obstacle repulsion forces, 76
oil spreading, 92

pedestrian decision-making, 27
pedestrian dynamics macroscopic
    levels, 29
pedestrian dynamics microscopic
    levels, 28

physical forces in skiing, 79
proxemic effect, 32

self-organization, 1
situated cellula agents, 36
slope edge repulsion forces, 77
Social Force Model, 32

The Intelligent Driver Model
     (IDM), 54

The Velocity-Dependent-
     Randomization (VDR),
     53
traffic modeling, 52

update schemes, 22

von Neumann neighborhood, 20

way-point forces, 74

Printed in the United States
by Baker & Taylor Publisher Services

Printed in the United States
by Baker & Taylor Publisher Services